GETTING MARRIED IN SCOTLAND

IONA McGREGOR

NMS Publishing Limited

Published by NMS Publishing Limited,
Royal Museum, Chambers Street, Edinburgh EH1 1JF

© I McGregor and NMS Publishing Limited 2000

Series editor: Iseabail Macleod

ISBN 1-901663-29-9

Other titles available in this series:

Building Railways	*Going to School*	*Scottish Bicycles and Tricycles*
Farming	*Going on Holiday*	*Scottish Engineering*
Feeding Scotland	*Going to Bed*	*Shipbuilding*
Fishing and Whaling	*Making Cars*	*Spinning and Weaving*
Leaving Scotland	*Scotland's Inland Waterways*	*Sporting Scotland*
Going to Church	*Scots in Sickness and Health*	

Forthcoming titles:

Going to the Pictures   *Scottish Showbusiness*

British Library Cataloguing in Publication Data
A catalogue record of this book
is available from the British Library.

ISBN 1 901663 29 9

Internal design layout by NMS Publishing Limited.
Cover design by Mark Blackadder.
Printed and bound in the United Kingdom by Bell and Bain Limited, Glasgow.

Contents

Acknowledgements

The author gratefully acknowledges assistance received from the Librarian of the School of Scottish Studies; and would also like to thank Mr and Mrs M Duck for permission to use the photograph on page 17.

Page 6 – 'O, I've been tae some great weddings!' comes from one of the interviews taped for the School of Scottish Studies by Margaret Bennett (1991), published in *Scottish Customs from the Cradle to the Grave*.

Page 33 – these ballads are taken from John Ord's *Bothy Songs and Ballads* (1930).

Page 87 – the 'Bride's Pie' recipe came from F Marian McNeill: *The Scots Kitchen*, originally published in 1929, quoted from the paperback version of the 2nd edition, 1963 (Mayflower, 1974).

Page 88 – David Allan, 'The Penny Wedding', from The National Gallery of Scotland.

Other illustrations: *page 10* (Aberdeen City Council – Arts and Recreation Department – Libraries); 14 (William Moir Bryce: *Holyrood – Its Palace and Its Abbey*, date and publisher not known); 17 (Pete Lindow, photographer; used by permission of Mr and Mrs M Duck).

Illustrations captioned '(SLA)' are from the Scottish Life Archive in the National Museums of Scotland.

Introduction

This book is intended to be more than an anthology of marriage customs, although details of that kind form a large part of it. It is also an enquiry into the social conditions and attitudes that influenced our forebears' choice of marriage partners and the legal system within which they made that choice. It examines the route to marriage, but not what happens after the wedding. Much of the material comes from the words of the people themselves.

The first two chapters look at the control of Kirk and State over Scottish marriage from the earliest times to our own day. The rest of the book deals with the practical problems of finding a marriage partner. The norms of society influence the search more than any other factor; and over the past three hundred years Scotland has seen enormous changes in lifestyle and population distribution as well as in the ethnic make-up of its people.

The Scots are both adaptable and tenacious of their history. In spite of the differences between 'then' and 'now' many customs have survived by fitting in with social changes. Nevertheless, the bulk of them, like the *Titanic*, have sunk into depths where we have to peer hard to make them out at all.

This book – intentionally – is a mixter-maxter conforming to the rhyme on what brides should wear to their wedding. I have tried to dig around the old quoted sources of information in the hope that every reader will find something new about Scottish wedding traditions. However, I acknowledge that I have borrowed freely from previous researchers. Here and there I have referred to practices that seem mild enough today, but have become obsolete because the prim Victorian age from which we draw almost all our modern wedding customs thought them much too blue.

Society has developed several institutions to keep itself stable and guarantee its survival from one generation to the next. The particular function of marriage is to control the relationships between men and women and so fend off disputes over property and inheritance. Marriage distinguishes itself from sexual partnership by drawing on the support of law and accepted social custom. Its definition has varied according to time and place, but all forms have evolved from the same assumption: the interests of the tribe must override individual wishes.

Because most people will sacrifice some degree of freedom to live in a well-ordered society, conformity – genuine or pretended – has been the norm, but accompanied by tensions and protest, in every age. Marriage impinges on the most intimate area of people's lives. Failure to match up to the ideal has generated social hypocrisy, individual heartbreak, and much of the world's greatest literature, from the *Iliad* to *Anna Karenina*.

Statistics suggest that the number of people getting married in Britain is on the decline, but marriage is more than an institution. Many of the social habits and expectations formerly attached to marriage have now bound themselves to more unofficial arrangements. The public seal of approval has taken on a distinctly commercial air, and those who do marry consider themselves entitled to privacy until the day of their wedding. In this we diverge sharply from our ancestors, who supervised and meddled at every stage from first meeting to the bedding of the bride.

Until the outbreak of World War II, Scottish marriage retained several features that had died out in the rest of the British islands. During the period immediately preceding that war, Scots law recognised three distinct forms of civil marriage as well as Jewish and Christian marriage in any of several denominations. Most of the civil varieties can be traced back to the earliest Christian period, perhaps even earlier. For our southern neighbours, 'Scotch marriage' was both a source of scandal and a way out of their own personal difficulties. This book will look at the way that marriage laws and customs have affected the people of Scotland since our history was first recorded.

'Oh, I've been tae some great weddings!'

1
In the Beginning

There is a scene that is duplicated up and down the land during the month of June. Outside a church in some Scottish town or village a small crowd has interrupted its daily affairs to gather on the pavement. Near the west door a dozen or so overdressed people are glancing furtively at their watches. The men seem a little self-conscious in their hired kilts; the women clutch at their wind-blown dresses and loudly admire each other's hats. They are all animated and voluble, yet at the same time curiously restrained. The crowd ignores them, barely stirring when they disappear into the church. Even the arrival of the groom rouses little excitement. These birds of paradise are not the main attraction. We are waiting for the bride.

Whatever her age or appearance, everyone will smile and murmur approval. By convention, all brides are beautiful. Nobody says so, but the spectators feel cheated unless she steps out of a beribboned limousine, dressed in white from head to toe. The nearer she matches their image, the greater their satisfaction. This event is not merely a wedding; it is a rite of passage, and such occasions are potentially dangerous. Participants must pay strict attention to detail. An untraditional bride destroys the magic.

When the crowd has dispersed, some bystanders will remain to watch the bride walk out of church on the arm of her groom. They are probably unaware of their compulsion to make sure that the ritual has been successfully accomplished. The guests troop out behind the happy couple and all reform on the pavement with a perceptible air of relief. A piper strikes up *Mairi's Wedding*, putting the photographer off his work. Before bride and groom lead their party to the reception, someone is sure to defy the minister and scatter forbidden confetti.

The particulars of this scene are modern; yet three elements are present that have existed since marriage in Scotland began – ancient Roman law redefined in a Christian context, Celtic tradition, and pagan folklore.

The first marriages in Scotland influenced by Roman law must have been those contracted by soldiers guarding Rome's Caledonian frontier. These foreign auxiliaries had been drawn into the army by the promise of

Roman citizenship if they survived to the end of their service. After they left the ranks, their children would be legitimised and their partners acquire the benefits of Roman marriage. These included inheritance rights and the protection of a legal code that ruled from Western Europe to the Euphrates. When Rome abandoned the province, the personnel of her remote encampments melted into the indigenous population.

Although traces of Christianity in Scotland date back to the third century AD, the new religion did not spread widely for another two hundred years. The Scottish Church remained largely Celtic in form until it was absorbed into the Roman discipline in the eleventh century. Even when Christianity was supposedly universal throughout the kingdom, older forms of non-Christian marriage survived.

Among the post-Roman inhabitants of Scotland, marriage sprang from an entirely different culture. There was a variety of different forms, collectively known as 'Celtic secular marriage'. The Roman historians, from Julius Caesar onwards, interpreted Celtic practices as unbridled polygamy, but this seems highly unlikely, even during the earliest period, given that all societies develop rules to avoid disputes over property and blood lines. Dio Cassius, a third-century historian, records a conversation between his contemporary, Julia Domna, wife of the Emperor Severus, and a high-born woman from Caledonia. She was probably detained at Rome as a hostage.

When the Empress reproached her guest with the promiscuous habits of her people, the Caledonian retorted that unlike Roman women, who affected monogamy and intrigued behind their husbands' backs, she and her compatriots were free to give themselves where they wished, and they gave themselves only to the best.

Allowing for the exaggeration of history written as rhetoric, this seems close to one of many types of sexual union or marriage recognised by the ancient Irish law tracts, all of them regulated in strict detail. By the seventh century AD, the original oral tradition had been committed to writing, and the practices that the Irish laws sanctioned – concubinage, divorce and polygamy – were in violent conflict with the decrees of the Church. Celtic secular marriage remained the norm in Ireland for Irish kings and nobles down to the seventeenth century, although occasionally disguised by a diplomatic request for the Pope to grant a dispensation to marry.

The ethnic connections between Ireland and Scotland are well known.

After the twelfth century, Celtic influence declined in the Lowlands, but in the Highlands and Islands a tribal society based on the ties of kinship survived into the seventeenth century. Laws and social customs were similar to those that flourished in Ireland. The history of Highland clans teems with disputes about succession and legitimacy which, scholars now claim, are evidence that Celtic secular marriage was still common in Scotland long after the Middle Ages.

The Church defined Christian marriage according to canon law, which was based on the law of ancient Rome. Marriage was available to anyone not in holy orders, provided he or she was not already married, did not intend to marry someone within the prohibited degrees of kinship, and had reached the age of twelve for women, or fourteen for men. These remained the legal ages for marriage in Scotland until 1929, when both were raised to sixteen.

Marriage was confirmed by an exchange of mutual consent. A betrothal ceremony known as handfasting preceded the wedding. The man and woman plighted their troth by joining hands, sometimes through a perforated stone.

A great deal of confusion has arisen from some older writers' use of the same word, 'handfasting', in contexts that variously mean betrothal, irregular legal marriage, or Celtic secular marriage.

On 24 July 1556 the Vicar of Aberdour handfasted the Earl of Bothwell's daughter to Robert Lawder. They repeated these words in front of him:

> I Robert Lawder tak thow Jane Hepburne to my spousit wyf as the law of the Haly Kirk schawis and thereto I plycht thow my trewht and syklyk I the said Jane Hepburne takis you Robert Lawder to my spousit husband as the law of the Haly Kirk schawis and thereto I plycht to thow my trewth.

The pre-Reformation wedding was a ceremony performed at the church door or marriage porch. There the bride was given away, usually by her father. She wore her hair hanging down her back as a symbol of virginity. This was described as being 'married in her hair'. The custom died out in the seventeenth century.

Again, a priest joined the couple's right hands, and they exchanged vows in almost the same words as at the handfasting. The priest then pronounced them man and wife '*per verba matrimonii de presenti*'. After

A good view of the South marriage porch of St Machar's Cathedral in Aberdeen.

the couple kissed, the husband presented his wife with her dower and morning gift, often money in an embroidered 'marriage purse'.

There was a prayer and benediction, and then everyone entered the church to take part in the bridal mass. In the early medieval period they would go to mass the following day, but in both cases the mass was never considered part of the marriage ceremony.

Although marriage was a Christian sacrament, unlike the others it was administered by the parties to each other, and did not need the intervention of a priest. Church doctrine taught that consent to 'carnal copulatioun, expremit by the wordis of the present tyme [*ie* 'I take thee … '], is the cause of matrimony'.

Pope Gregory IX had already declared in 1236 that a promise of marriage followed by sexual intercourse constituted a valid union. This was known as marriage '*per verba de futuro*', and it was the origin of one form of 'Scotch marriage'.

The Church never reneged on this ruling, although it deplored the consequences. Its disapproval had less to do with carnality than with fear of incestuous marriage – an all-too-likely hazard among static rural communities. In the early thirteenth century Pope Innocent III imposed the calling of banns on all Christian marriages (a practice that lasted until 1977 in Scotland) to allow time for questions of kinship to be investigated. Dispensations were available from the Holy See, at a price.

The number of handfasted couples who proceeded to live as man and wife presented the Church with a serious problem. Church statutes decreed that all betrothals and marriages must be carried out by a priest, and in public, while betrothed couples were exhorted to abstain from intercourse until after their wedding. The Council of Trent decreed that marriage was invalid unless performed by a priest in front of at least three adult male witnesses. None of this reduced the numbers that refused to advance from betrothal to wedding, and the habit of marriage '*per verba de futuro*' continued to spread at all levels of society.

No doubt many couples did take the 'Why bother?' attitude, and the similarity of wording in wedding and betrothal ceremonies must have led to genuine mistakes; but there could be other reasons for the delay. The remoteness of many rural areas made it difficult to follow up a declaration of intent to marry with an immediate church service. The minister of Eskdale wrote about his own parish for Sir John Sinclair's *Statistical Account of Scotland* in the late eighteenth century:

> That piece of ground at the meeting of the Black and White Esks was remarkable in former times for an annual fair [where] ... it was the custom for unmarried persons of both sexes to choose a companion ... with whom they were to live till that time next year. This was called hand fasting, or hand in fist. If they were pleased with each other at that time, then they continued together for life; if not, they separated, and were free to make another choice as at the first. The fruit of their connexion (if there were any), was always attached to the disaffected person. In later times, when this part of the country belonged to the abbacy of Melrose, a priest to whom they gave the name of Book i' bosom (either because he carried in his bosom a bible, or, perhaps a register of the marriages), came from time to time to confirm the marriages.

The couples mentioned were of course still legally married when they parted, and any further unions they contracted would be bigamous.

The uncertainties of life in a turbulent age provide another reason for handfasted marriage. In 1482, for example, during a dispute about the ownership of Kilravock castle, a certain Donald Mackintosh undertook to capture and occupy the castle on behalf of Lauchlane Mackintosh and, as a pledge of good faith, promised to marry Lauchlane's daughter. Since the two were within the forbidden degrees of kinship, Lauchlane agreed to seek a dispensation from Rome at his own expense. The marriage contract ensured that the two men would remain loyal to each other, but their plan was too hazardous for them to wait until the dispensation arrived:

> And als sone as ye said castell beys tane be ye saide Donalde, the said Lauchlane sal gar incontinent, bot [without] ony langer delay, handfast Margret his saide dochter, with the saide Donalde, and ly with him as scho war his lauchfull wiff; Ande als sone as the dispensacione cumys hame, the saide Donald is oblist incontinent but ony langer delay, to mary and spous the saide Margret, and to haude her in honour and worship at all his power as his weddit wiff, for all the days of his lyff.

In its anxiety to avoid incest, by the seventh century AD the Church had extended its prohibitions on marriage to the seventh degree of consanguinity or affinity (relationship through marriage). In 1215 the Lateran Council was forced to relax the prohibitions to the fourth degree, but ingenious complications developed. Those who stood sponsors at the baptism of infants were deemed to have acquired '*cognatio spiritualis*' (kinship of the spirit) both between themselves and between themselves and the families of the infants' parents. The result was matrimonial gridlock. Only the Pope could grant dispensations for kinsfolk to marry, and they were expensive. No wonder so many couples or their parents took the shortcut '*per verba de futuro*'.

In 1554 Archbishop Hamilton of St Andrews wrote despairingly that it was almost impossible to find two well-born people in Scotland who could be married without a dispensation. He managed to wrest a concession from Rome that the Papal legate in Scotland might waive the prohibitions for baptismal sponsors and kinsfolk down to the third degree. In practice this worked through a block grant of dispensations from Rome, which could then be used as needed.

The medieval Church did not follow Roman law in permitting divorce. Once two people were married, they could not separate except on grounds of adultery or attempted murder of one spouse by another. Even then, their union was for life and they could not marry anyone else – a position still maintained in official Roman Catholic doctrine. The only other way out was through annulment, which also had to be granted by the Pope. As is well known, Henry VIII's impatience with this situation led to the English Reformation.

The Church's concern with prohibited degrees may seem faintly ridiculous today (although there is still a long list of barred relationships); what is more repugnant to modern thinking is the fact that marriage was permitted at the onset of puberty. We must however remember that most people would not have contemplated getting married until much later than the legal age. For men, at least, having to support a family would make this inevitable. The time chosen related less to everyday reality than to the Church's pessimistic view of human nature. As far as it was concerned, it was better for adolescents to marry than to burn.

Among the nobility and royal houses of Europe, marriage was a means of cementing dynastic and political alliances, with the betrothal or marriage contract often agreed soon after birth. Another inducement towards early marriage was the 'merchet', a penalty that a feudal superior could claim on the marriage of a ward. 'Consent' can hardly have entered into the unions that parents made on behalf of their children.

At the highest level of society, marriages were often made by proxy. Margaret Tudor, daughter of King Henry VII of England, was married to James IV's proxy, the Earl of Bothwell, on 25 January 1502. They were related in the fourth degree, and so had to seek a papal dispensation. She was then twelve or thirteen years old. James himself was twenty-eight. A year later, Margaret's mother died; forbidding any sign of mourning, King Henry went ahead with arrangements to send his daughter to Scotland. She travelled north that summer with an escort of more than five hundred attendants. James met her at Dalkeith on 3 August. While waiting for him, Margaret had lost some of her favourite horses in a stable fire and her mind was more on her loss than on the impending marriage. The wedding took place on 8 August at Holyrood Abbey.

John Younge, Somerset Herald, describes the magnificent preparations for Margaret's entry into Edinburgh, followed by the marriage at Holyrood Abbey. Since this was a royal wedding, the ceremony took place inside the Abbey church, but not at the altar. The Queen's party were on the left side, near the font; the King's on the right:

The Kyng was in a Gowne of Whit Damaske figured with Gold and lynned with Sarcenet … a Dowblet of Cloth of Gold, and a Payre of Scarlette Hosys … hys Bonnet Blak, with a ryche Balay [ruby] and his Swerde about hym.

Margaret wore:

a rich Robbe … borded of Cramsyn Velvet … Sche had a varey riche Coller of Gold, of Pyerrery [jewels] and Perles, round her neck, and the Croune upon hyr Hed; Her hayre hangyng. Betwixt the said Croune and the Hayres was a varey riche coyfe hangyng downe behynde the whole Length of the Body.

They were married by the Archbishop of Glasgow, after the Archbishop of York had read out the papal dispensation:

Thys doon, the Trumpets blew for Joy; and the King, being bareheded and holdyng her by the Ryght Haund, was conveyd … to the Hygh Awter. Before the wich was drest a Place for them Two to knell apon ryches Cushyns of Cloth of Gold … abydynge there during the Tyme of the Masse. At the Gospel they maid their Offryng, and before the Saunt Canon she was anoynted. After wich the Kynge gafe hyr the Septre in hyr Hand.

A view into Holyrood Abbey where King James IV married Margaret Tudor.

2
'The Blessed Ordinance of God'

After the Reformation, the newly constituted Kirk of Scotland faced many perplexing questions concerning marriage. The solutions found did not all appear at the same time, nor were they applied consistently throughout the country. During more than one hundred years identical decisions appear in the records so frequently that we have to conclude that large numbers of people disregarded the decrees of both General Assembly and Kirk Session and clung as far as possible to their former habits.

In the main, the Kirk tried to enforce the same rules as its predecessor. There was a minimum age for marriage; wedding ceremonies had to be conducted by a minister before the congregation after the three-fold proclamation of banns; and only those who met the necessary conditions could marry. The first General Assembly reduced the prohibited degrees to a list drawn from chapter eighteen of Leviticus – a practical necessity after dispensations were abolished.

Since marriage was no longer a sacrament, ordinary courts of law could grant divorce. At first this was only available on grounds of adultery, but desertion for four years was added in 1573. A Commissary Court began to deal with all matters nowadays covered by family legislation. Its history of case law shaped the form of Scottish marriage until 1830, when its duties devolved to the Court of Session.

Although the 1560 *Buke of Discipline* took a stern line on adultery, demanding the death penalty for guilty parties, it was never enforced. Church courts had no power to inflict a capital sentence, and the civil authorities balked at such severity. Like political parties challenged about their sinking status in the polls, the Church put on a brave face:

> Yf the Civile Sweard [sword] foolischelie spair the lyeff of the offendar yit may not the Churche be negligent in thair office, which is to excommunicat the wicked and … pronunce the innocent partie to be at freedome.

Yet in practice the Kirk received back adulterers, 'gyf the fructis [fruits] of repentance of long tyme appeir in thame'. They could even hope for a

Miss Fiona Lowther and Lt Malcolm Duck RM at their wedding in the Canongate Kirk, Edinburgh, 14 October 1989. (Pete Lindow)

second marriage. 'Yf thai can not leve [live] continent … , we can not forbid thame to use the remeady ordained of God.'

By 1600, presumably with known examples in mind, the Assembly realised it had provided a charter for people dissatisfied with their current spouses, and asked the Convention of Estates to pass an Act discharging all marriages 'of such persons as are convicted of adultery'.

The modern Church of Scotland restored the right of divorced persons to be married in church in 1959.

The most striking feature of the post-Reformation Church was the enormous power it put into the hands of local Kirk Sessions. Over time one was set up in every parish. The Sessions were under the jurisdiction of Presbyteries, Synods and the General Assembly, but this applied only in broad principle. In practice they claimed the right to direct the everyday life of the people in minutest detail. They were composed of men important in their own area, such as merchants and local gentry. In the small Scottish burghs their membership often overlapped that of the Town Council. Session Registers and Burgh Records echo each other's concerns.

The specific duty of the Kirk Session was to keep a brotherly eye on the backsliding of fellow citizens, high and low, and occasionally this included the minister himself. Until well into the nineteenth century they continued to supervise private lives – or tried to supervise them – to an extent that would be intolerable to a generation accustomed to personal freedom. Conservative social attitudes and the small-town structure of much of Scottish society reinforced their meddling.

Popular attention has fixed on the Session's prurient zeal in compelling those guilty of fornication to appear on the stool of penitence during divine service. This is an accurate but limited view of its activities. Its scrutiny went much farther. In any case, judging by the multitude of entries, public humiliation failed, both as a deterrent and as a threat to social reputation. Congregations seem to have kept their eyes discreetly averted. In 1655, when some English soldiers were quartered in Glasgow, the Session resolved that: ' … so long as the English continue in the toun they will put no person on the pillar because they mock at them.'

Session Registers carry many entries about couples fined and disciplined for not proceeding to marriage after their betrothal. At a wedding ceremony after the Reformation the minister affirmed the couple's marriage, but he did not make the marriage itself. That was based on the act of mutual consent, first pronounced at the betrothal or handfasting. In the eyes of the law handfasting followed by sexual union still constituted a valid marriage. Like the Roman Catholic Church, the Kirk deeply disapproved, but was not able to eradicate the fixed habit of centuries. In 1575 the General Assembly suggested that those who wished to betroth themselves should merely give in their names to the Session, and not make their promises until the marriage ceremony. This seems not to have dissipated the confusion between betrothal and marriage vows, nor discouraged those who simply could not be bothered. Frequently, couples approached the minister only when they wished to baptise their first child. The Session usually agreed to the marriage if the couple promised to pay a fine and make a public act of repentance. Many entries in the Kirk Session Registers lamenting 'fornicacioune' are, in fact, examples of irregular marriage.

At a later date, another great disincentive to regular marriage was the Session Clerk's fee for an entry in the Register. There was also a charge for proclaiming the banns (larger if read all together, rather than on three successive Sundays). Fines for not getting married in church continued to be imposed right through the eighteenth century. After the early 1800s the punishment dwindled to a public rebuke, and in the Victorian era the Session administered this privately rather than in church.

Parental consent to the marriage was a social courtesy expected of those of any age, while their parents lived. It had never been a legal requirement for anyone deemed old enough to marry. This was something else the Reformers tried to change, but as the *Buke of Discipline* shows they tempered their efforts with common sense and even sympathy towards young couples wanting to marry:

> Yf the father, freind, or maister, ganestand thair requeast, and have na other caus then … lack of guidis, or … [because they] ar nott so hyght-born as thai requyre … the Ministerie or Magistrat may enter in the place of the parent, and … may admit thame to mariage: for the work of God aught not to be hyndered by the corrupt affectionis of worldlie men. The work of God we call, when two heartis (without filthynes before committit) ar so joyned, that boyth … ar content to live together in that holy band of Matrimonye.

In dealing with single mothers, the Kirk Session proved to be much more effective than the modern Child Support Agency. It went farther than upholding a claim for maintenance – the father of the child could be forced to marry the mother. If she relinquished her right to marriage, he was obliged to compensate her with a dowry, and be responsible for rearing their child. The following case is typical:

> 11 April 1565 James Adeson in Arneill and Elizabeth Boy … accused of fornicacione, manifestit be procreacion of ane child betuix them. Thai confes. Elizabeth clamis mariaig of James, according to the law of God, for defloracion of hir virginite; finale, sche, behaldyng he culd nocht be persuadit wyllingle tharto, grantis to accep ane porcion of hys gayr to help to dot hyr, and quitis and renuncis mariage of him, sche being dischergit of the burdyng and educacion of thar barne. And James oblesis hym to resave the barn, and to accept upon hym the educacion [bringing up] and expens of the barn, and to pay x lib. to Elizabeth, tharof v lib. in hand, and fynd caucion for the other v lib. accitat: quhilk Elizabeth accepis and exoners James of mariaige. And bayth the saidis parteis ar ordenit to mak public satisfaccion in the assemble of the congregacion this nixt Sundaye.

The minister and elders could refuse marriage to those they disapproved of – bankruptcy, scandalous behaviour, and not being able to recite the Creed, the Commandments and the Lord's Prayer were among reasons cited. On the other hand, they dealt severely with those who contracted to marry and then changed their minds. Unless there was some grave impediment, such as a previous claim on either partner, the Session would order them to get married forthwith, whether sexual intercourse had followed the handfasting or not, and even if the couple had made the contract in private and both now regretted it. If necessary, the Session called in the civil arm of the law.

There are many examples to illustrate that old Scots proverb, 'Sudden friendship's sure repentance'. The following extract from the Burgh Records of Newburgh demonstrates that even after the Act of Union the handfasting contract or betrothal still carried more weight than the wedding ceremony. The latter was, so to speak, only the icing on the cake:

> 1709 May 19. Gavin Spens lait Bailie ther [Newburgh] gave in ane complaint upon Katharin Baxter that whereas ther was depositat in his hands with consent, ane contract of marriage betwixt her and James Imbrie, and the said Katharin desyring to hear the said contract read, she violently took the said contract out of the hands of John Houg tennant in Mugdrum, whom she brought along to read it, and she brunt the samen .... The Baillies appoints the said Katharin to be confynd to the Tolbooth till sutch tyme as she shall ... return to her husband, James Imbrie, and cohabit with him.

Faced with this threat, Katharin made up the contract anew, and was escorted to James Imbrie's house.

The Newburgh Bailies (magistrates) were as hostile as the Kirk to the 'deboshry' of 'piping and dancing and profane minstrelling' at local weddings. As late as 1726 they imposed heavy fines on couples who invited more than eight non-family guests.

The Session examined all pleas with thoroughness and impartiality before pronouncing judgement. If no witnesses were available, the parties were put on their oath. When someone objected to a marriage (usually on the grounds of a prior contract) the Session would set a day to investigate the claim. If the claimant failed to turn up, the marriage could go ahead.

The Session was also aware that children and young adults could be pressured into marriage against their will. There was one remarkable early case of this kind at St Andrews. The Kirk Session summoned James Beynston and Johanna Hepburn, one of the ten natural children of the former Bishop of Moray, to order them to 'procead to solemnizacion of thar mariaige, contract betuix tham detfully wyth consent of thar parentis and publeist be proclamacion of thar bannis'.

Joanna claimed that her brother, the parson of Kynoyr, had forced her consent. He had brought her on horseback from Perth to Stravithie, threatening that: 'gyf I consentit nocht to the said promys ... he sudd drown me in the watter of Erne as I past to Perth. And I beand bot ane yong woman of xiij or xiiij yearis of aige ... bursting owt wyth tearis ... beand far fra my freindis at that tym ... wes compellit to consent'.

Turning to the intended husband, the Session heard a similar story:

> James Beynston confessis that ... his father commandit hym to consent tharto, or ellis he suld never get ... nan of his heretaige; and sua ...he consentit, albeid the sayd Joanna apperit to hym to have als lytell wyll of hym as he had of hyr.

Johanna had a good lawyer, and was able to produce witnesses to the truth of her story:

> Wyliam Cwnygham ... hard Patrik Hepburn say to Joanna, his syster, gyf sche wald nocht consent ... sche suld never get gud of hyr father bot gang lyik ane huyr [whore].
>
> Wyliam Lewrmonth, familiar servand to Patrik, Bischop of Murray ... be his ayth deponis that ... Joanna Hepburn, at hyr cuming fra Sanct Jhonstoun [Perth] to Strawethy, had na consent of hyr father and wes dissavit [deceived] be ... hyr brother that brocht hyr.
>
> Jssobel Morton, Lady of Bernis ... deponis that she hard Joanna Hepburn say ... that ... hyr brother brocht hyr thar aganis hyr wyll fra Sanct Johnstoun upon ane hors behynd hym ... and ... saw at that self sam tym Joanna ... burst owt wyth greting and tearis; quhilk seyn be the deponar, sche departit fra tham, beand desparit of ony gud succes to follow upon sic begynnyn.

Satisfied by this evidence, the Session released James and Joanna from their marriage contract. No one had appeared to uphold it, and the presence of the ex-Bishop's servant suggests that Patrick Hepburn (guardian of Queen Mary's Bothwell) may have instigated the proceedings – one good deed in his disreputable life.

The fines that the Kirk Sessions imposed on those who had contracted irregular marriages were adjusted according to income. For a nobleman they could rise as high as one thousand pounds Scots.

At one time an irregular marriage was a marriage performed outside the parish of residence, but the term later covered marriages performed by Episcopalian and Roman Catholic priests, as well as those by barred or dissenting ministers from the increasingly fragmented Presbyterian Church. The imposition of Episcopacy in the seventeenth century for a time reversed the situation.

The reason the Session disliked its flock getting married outside the parish was pecuniary as well as religious. In 1579 the Reformers had tried to institute a system to relieve want that would not be dependent on charity. However, the battle to enforce legal assessment of a poor rate on individuals only began to be won from 1845 onwards. Until then, city hospitals and Kirk Sessions had to deal with the problem out of their own funds. In keeping weddings on home territory, the Session had in mind the sellers of food and drink within their own parish:

> 1653 Januar 9 .... Sundrie women of this parochine [Newburgh] ... goeth to other Kirks to perfyt and accomplish thair promise of marriage, whairby ye poor of this parochin are prejudged, the selleris of aill, bread, flesh and other victuals are damnified. Thairfor ye Session ... hes ordained whosoever ... shall goe to ony other church for the effect foirsaid they shall pay ten merkes usuall money of this realme.

Similarly, in 1608, the Town Council of Stirling ruled that 'all wedding parties sall mak thair brythellis and banquetis within this burgh fra this furth'. The brythell, or bridal – *ie* 'bride ale' – was the celebration that followed the wedding. The Session tried to strike a balance between commercial interests and fear that the revelry might get out of hand. This was all the more likely in that bridals were now the main outlet for all the feasting and drinking once associated with saints' days and other medieval Church festivals. The Kirk tried to restrict the amount of money that might be spent on the bridal and the permitted number of guests. Those fined for breaking the regulations were usually the proprietors of ale-houses where the bridal was held, but in 1688 the Presbytery of Peebles fined a minister, Mr John Hay, for overstepping the limit when he married a couple in his own home. This is an early example of the 'house wedding' that became standard in the next century.

The Kirk's denunciation of former amusements stirred up great resentment among the people. It was particularly ill-disposed towards piping and dancing because of their perceived connection with popery. This eventually resulted in a change to the customary times for weddings. At first, marriage was always celebrated on a Sunday. There was a short service at noon, either preceding or following divine worship. Sometimes the bridal guests were disinclined to return to church for the afternoon service. St Andrews Kirk Session appealed to the magistrates to help them restrain

the grite abuse usit be new mareit personis in violatioun of the Sabbat day; and in spetial quhen, the day of thair mareage eftir nuin, they resort nocht to hering of the doctrine, and at evin eftir supper insolentlie … perturbis the town wytht rynning thair throw in menstralye and harlatrye.

The permissible days for marriage were extended to Wednesdays and Fridays, and then to any day of the week, provided there were sufficient witnesses. Finally, marriage on a Sunday was forbidden. The chosen day varied in different parts of the country, as we shall see.

Over time, the Kirk Session was forced to relax its control over those wishing to marry. The causes were many – they included the rise of Moderatism in the Church of Scotland and the sheer growth of population, particularly in the expanding industrial cities. Society in general, increasingly sophisticated and secularised, became less willing to accept the moral direction of the Kirk, even when it continued to fill the church pews. In addition, the nation's increased prosperity accompanied a steady widening of class differences. Paradoxically, the Kirk Session was a better promoter of democracy when at its most tyrannical. At a later stage, it became less quick to chastise sinners without fear or favour.

In eighteenth-century Scotland, rates of irregular marriage began to increase, promoting a movement to remove some of the underlying causes. Episcopalian marriage had been brought within the fold of respectability from 1712, and an Act of 1834 legalised marriages performed by all other Christian denominations. The Kirk expected these measures to remove the need for all forms of irregular marriage. Others factors, to be discussed later, thwarted their intentions. In 1865 the Westminster Parliament set up a Royal Commission to examine the state of marriage in Britain. One of its aims was to persuade the Scots to give up their peculiar marriage customs. The Commission came up against stubborn opposition, partly based on a feeling that it was trying to impose English marriage law. The Free Church argued that Scottish custom was a great safeguard against concubinage and illegitimacy, and prevented the seducer from leaving a woman to dishonour and ruin. (Under Scots law, the subsequent marriage of their parents legitimised children born out of wedlock.) The Established Church supported their brethren, although not in such colourful language. There were several sharp exchanges – the Commission told the ministers that they were in no position to determine whether irregular marriage was salutary or otherwise, while the Scottish Churches claimed that seduction and bigamy were more endemic in England, and were sceptical about the Commission's reassurance that it did not intend to abolish the right of legitimisation after marriage.

The Lord Justice General supported the Churches' stand and refused to accept the Commission's findings – in the event, the only noteworthy change introduced was the Marriage Notice (Scotland) Act of 1878, which required written notice of intended marriages to be posted on the Registrar's door. The Established Church continued to insist on a monopoly over the publishing of banns, for which it charged steeply – a great source of grievance to the other Scottish Churches.

Civil marriage became available in France from 1792, in England from 1836, and in Germany from 1875, but it was not available in Scotland on the same footing until 1939. Until then there were various hybrid forms of registration. In 1854 a small fine began to be imposed for contracting an irregular marriage. This was only a device to secure registration, and the fine was abolished in 1856, when the office of Registrar appeared. Couples could also register a 'Rutherglen marriage', an artificial absurdity, whereby they would appear before a magistrate who, for a fee, would record their marriage and issue a certificate. The certificate passed as unofficial 'marriage lines', and many believed that 'going before the shirra' constituted a regular marriage. Lord Cockburn, in his *Circuit Journeys*, writes about a Justice of the Peace in Lanarkshire, who unabashedly confessed to having issued over twelve hundred certificates within ten years. He was paid in half-crowns (approximately 18 p) or, failing that, a dram of whisky!

In all these variations, the certificate was only a receipt for the fine or quasi-fine the official demanded. In 1939 a marriage act established official Registry marriages in Scotland, and finally swept away both marriage established by declaration and by the promise of marriage followed by sexual relations. Marriage 'by habit and repute' remains, but has been superfluous since family law began to validate the rights and responsibilities of those who co-habit without regular marriage.

3
Meeting and Courting

Cinderella and King Cophetua are exceptions proving the rule that the majority of people seek a marriage partner within their own age-range, with background and expectations broadly similar to their own. 'Better marry ower the midden than ower the muir,' says the Scots proverb, and its basic idea – that like fits best with like – applies even when partners originate from different geographical areas. Those marrying for the second time frequently repeat a familiar pattern.

Nowadays men and women can seek each other out through media that were unimaginable fifty years ago – the Internet and telephone chat lines are obvious examples. Others, such as newspaper advertisements, clubs, singles bars and dating agencies are not exactly new, but either exist in an updated form or have become socially acceptable as a means of pairing people off. Another development has transformed the large company office into a more gender-balanced environment. Today's young women do not wait to be asked. Vernacular literature makes it clear that Scotswomen have never been 'blate' in going after their chosen man, but it once was middle-class dogma passed from mother to daughter that nice girls waited to be wooed.

How did our ancestors make contact?

People have always exploited institutions ostensibly set up for some other purpose. Going to church is not a purely religious activity. In a late fifteenth-century poem, 'The Tretis of the Tua Mariit Wemen and the Wedo', the widow artfully draws attention to herself by displaying the gold-illuminated 'bright buke' on her knee as she sizes up possibilities with her cloak drawn over her face. Already bored with her husband, one of the young wives wishes she could look for a new lover every year at 'playis, and … preichingis, and pilgrimages greit'.

These meeting places were open to all except the few who lived in isolated areas. Medieval communities were too small to create any sharp difference of lifestyle between town and country. With the exception of ale-wives and burghers' widows, who might continue to direct their

husband's business, townswomen did not usually work alongside men as they did in rural areas. Nevertheless, the workshop-based economy and modest size of most Scottish burghs precluded any rigid separation between craftsmen and other townsfolk even during their working day. Men and women met freely in the daily business of life, in circumstances that lasted for several hundred years.

All this began to change towards the middle of the eighteenth century with the beginning of the industrial age. The expanding cities became even more attractive to those seeking work or amusement. Elizabeth Spence, who travelled round Scotland shortly before 1820, visited Glasgow during the week of the annual fair. She noted:

Groups of *lassies*, all smartly drest, but all without caps, and many, till they enter the city, without shoes or stockings, walking nicely attired, with all their clothes carefully pinned up, treading along with the most perfect unconcern, and full of pleasing anticipations of the joys of the fair .... The chief amusement seems to be walking through the streets until evening, when the public-houses are filled with the holiday people, who dance till day-light to the sound of the bagpipe.

With the arrival of widespread industrialisation, the population spread changed dramatically. In the middle of the eighteenth century nearly two-thirds of Scotland's inhabitants (one and a quarter million) lived in the Highlands and Southern Uplands; by 1976, seventy-five per cent were crammed into the Central Belt. This unbalanced distribution was well under way by the Victorian age.

Most young women who entered the urban workforce did so either as factory hands or domestic servants, with a smaller proportion being taken on as shop assistants. In all these occupations the sexes were in effect segregated during the working day. The female employees in the jute and cotton mills vastly outnumbered the male foremen who supervised them. House servants enjoyed a more comfortable existence, but if they slept at their place of work they lived in virtual slavery. As well as extorting the maximum amount of work, employers did their best to keep their maid-servants away from men. Alfred List wrote in 1861:

> The cry everywhere is 'No followers!' as if the young serving girl had no title to love or be loved … as if it were her sole duty to waste existence in minis-tering to the wants of others.

With the curious double vision of so many of his contemporaries, he exhorted mistresses to keep all house keys on their toilet tables when they went to bed, otherwise

> you may never know what junketings are going on below …. Satan is never busier than at night.

Domestic service absorbed huge numbers of girls from the age of twelve upwards, and their numbers increased during the nineteenth century when the desire to demonstrate middle-class status trickled down to families on small incomes. The wealthy could afford to take on male servants as butlers or footmen, but this provided few opportunities to find a partner. Unless the master or mistress was exceptionally enlightened, romantic connections between servants working in the same household were strictly forbidden. They could count themselves lucky if they had a few free hours each week to go out and pursue the search. Although the situation had relaxed a little by the early twentieth century, domestic service fell increasingly out of favour, and after Word War II housemaids disappeared from all but the wealthiest households.

Courting was a near impossibility in the cramped conditions of working-class housing, so lovers usually met outside the home. From the mid-nineteenth century onwards train and steamer excursions became a

Domestic service provided little opportunity for young women to socialise with the opposite sex. (SLA)

popular holiday pastime, especially during the local 'fair weeks' or trades holidays. The old photographs of people dancing and singing on the crowded decks give an erroneous impression of leisure. 'Doon the watter' on board a Clyde steamer was not for every day. For families it was a short respite from the hard grind of work, and for the young an opportunity to strike up acquaintance with someone special.

In the Victorian and Edwardian eras the larger Scottish cities supported music halls and theatres, popular both for their entertainment value and the hope of chance encounters. Dance halls ceased to be disreputable in the early part of the twentieth century. Glasgow, in particular, was known for its addiction to dancing and the cinema, which became a medium of mass entertainment in the 1930s. 'Dancing and the search for a mate go hand in hand,' stated one of the Carnegie United Kingdom Trust Reports in 1943.

Those who could not afford to buy an entry ticket for the dance hall paraded up and down certain streets after work, just like Elizabeth Spence's 'lassies' a hundred years before them, in the same way as people take an evening stroll in Mediterranean ports and cities.

The dance hall had its own self-enforcing etiquette – to violate it would bring scorn from the very person some infatuated young man or woman was trying to impress. Going with someone to the cinema meant that progress had been made. In the smoke-filled filmhouses of the 1940s and 50s, those who really wanted to see the main film left the back rows free for courting couples. Some cinemas provided double seats, more expensive than their neighbours in the same row. In Dundee they were advertised at the box-office as 'Golden Baskets'.

Before World War II the numerical possibilities of enjoying a romantic encounter were much greater for country-dwellers than nowadays. In the Scottish Lowlands both north and south of the Forth, arable farming remained highly labour-intensive until well into the twentieth century. Men and women did different kinds of work, but the majority of farms employed both.

Apart from the workers employed all year round, seasonal activities such as tattie howking (potato harvesting), corn shearing, and soft fruit picking in the Blairgowrie area, brought in itinerant hordes from the West Highlands or as far away as Ireland. Mr and Mrs Burke met on a Lothian harvest field shortly before they settled in a doss-house near Edinburgh's Grassmarket and began selling their fellow lodgers to the anatomist, Dr Knox.

Until the introduction of the mowing scythe, which needed a strong man to wield it, young women sheared the corn with small hand-sickles, taking ten hours to reap one third of an acre. Other harvesters gathered the corn and tied it into sheaves with bands of plaited straw. Let Robert Burns take up the tale:

> You know our country custom of coupling a man and a woman together as part-
> ners in the labours of harvest. In my fifteenth year my partner was a bewitching
> creature, a year younger than myself … a bonnie, sweet, sonsie lass. In short, she
> … initiated me in that delicious passion, which … I hold to be the first of human
> joys …. I never expressly said I loved her. Indeed, I did not know myself why
> I liked so much to loiter behind with her when returning in the evening from our
> labours … why my pulse beat such a furious ratan, when I looked and fingered
> over her little hand, to pick out the cruel nettle-stings and thistles.

In Burns's day, the young country women would meet at night for a 'rocking', equivalent to the modern sewing-bee. They would sit in the barn or farmhouse kitchen, spinning their wool and flax with a distaff and spindle. Story telling and music lightened their task, and after the meeting broke up, the young men would escort them home across 'the rigs o' barley' – with all the opportunities and consequences described in Burns's own lyrics. The rockings died out when distaff and spindle gave way to the spinning wheel. Even the most ardent wooer would find that a heavy burden to carry across the fields.

Something similar to Ayrshire rockings happened in Shetland. The young women would meet at each house in turn to prepare the wool for spinning and work until nine or ten in the evening, then the lads would arrive to chat with them. Wool and caird (wool carder) were laid aside, the fiddle came down off the wall, and the floor was cleared for dancing. At three o'clock in the morning, the meeting broke up. Those who could walked home, and the rest lay down – men and women indiscriminately – on a shakedown in the barn until breakfast. In 1837 *The Shetland Journal* published an article in defence of the sleeping arrangements, implying that the 'cairdings' continued.

There were other social opportunities at the country fairs, many of which dated from long before the Reformation. Their heyday was in the eighteenth and early nineteenth centuries; they continued on a reduced scale even when it became normal practice to move livestock by rail. Those dedicated to labourers looking for work were known as 'hiring-fairs' or 'feeing-markets', but goods and beasts were on sale as well. They attracted hawkers, fiddlers, conjurors and scores of small traders, as well as those in search of strong drink or a sexual partner. Here are a few of them:

Edinburgh	All Hallows in November
Peebles	Beltane Fair in May
Fife-Pitlessie	Fife-Pitlessie Fair in May and October
Aberdeen	Timmer Fair in October
Biggar	Seed Thursday in March
Old Cumnock (Ayrshire)	Scythe Fair in July

Artists such as David Wilkie, James Howe and Walter Geikie caught the exhilaration and lively atmosphere of the fairs on their canvases.

The harvest suppers of the North-East were reputed to be among the most abandoned occasions of the farming year. They ended with a traditional drink:

> The concoction that brought the event to an almost bacchanalian ferment and made sure that any farmer with a very genteel wife or daughter took her home early … was handed down in the generations …. Its potency was something proverbial … it led to goodness knows what kind of indiscretions and sometimes to open carnality.

A poet later than Burns gives the general recipe as:

> A coggie o' yill [ale] and a pickle ait [oat] meal,
>   And a dainty wee drappie o' whisky.

In the latter half of the eighteenth century, more efficient methods of agriculture led to the abolition of the old runrig system in favour of enclosures and larger farms. The smallholders who had cultivated the land since the Middle Ages did not disappear, but they were largely replaced by paid farmservants hired on six-month contracts. The married farm workers were known as cottars; they received a tied cottage in return for work on the land. (A frequently imposed condition was that their wives would work in the dairy.) Cottars, as well as single farmhands, might move on at the end of their terms, fixed at 28 May and 28 November, although in their case it was more usual to remain for a full year. The motivation was often a search for better accommodation or working conditions. Most of the farmworkers would circulate within something like a twenty-mile radius.

This increase in social interaction was offset by the development of mechanised farming. From 1850 onwards the number of outdoor women workers began to decline throughout most parts of Scotland. An exception was the Lothian region, where the male farmhands or hinds were hired on condition that they brought with them women workers known as 'bondagers'. This system lingered on until World War II.

By the mid-nineteenth century the majority of male farm-hands in both southern and northern Scotland were single men. They ate and slept in barrack-like stone huts known as bothies, with the minimum of comforts. In some areas, accommodation was over a stable, known as a 'chaumer'. A farmhand might take six to eight years to save enough to marry and rent a two-horse farm. Many would never achieve this. Farmers grudged the expense of building new housing, and married workers without a cottage would use the bothies during their working week. They would see their families in some neighbouring village one day per week at the most.

On smaller farms, a kindlier relationship between farmer and men might still exist, but in the larger establishments there was now a marked social divide between employer and employed. The bothy lads were not

'What the butler saw' – an old postcard showing a courting couple on their best behaviour; date and source unknown. (SLA)

BE GOOD, AND IF YOU CAN'T BE GOOD, BE CAREFUL

welcome in the farm kitchen. They expressed their feelings about the harsh conditions in the 'bothy ballads', naming and shaming their grasping taskmasters and singing of their search for love and sex:

> As I gaed in by Monymusk,
> The moon was shinin' clear;
> As I held on to Lethendy
> To see my Maggie dear.

Sexual encounters rather than wooing are the main theme of the love songs. The farm lads roamed the countryside at night and knocked to be let into their sweethearts' bedrooms. By now it was usually the kitchen lass who was being pursued, and she slept in the farmhouse. The lovers' tryst did not always go according to plan:

> I did gang, when I did think
> That a' were sleeping soun';
> But plague upon yon auld wife,
> For she cam' slinkin' doun ....

> And when she saw I wadna slip
> She ran to the gudeman, [farmer]
> Says:– 'There's a lad into the house,
> And that I winna stan'.'

> For it is a most disgraceful thing,
> It would provoke a saunt, [saint]
> To see a' the servant girls wi' lads
> When the gentle anes maun want. [ones; go without]

Discovery could result in dismissal for both servant lass and ploughman, but there was a recommended precaution. The farmer's eldest daughter was known as 'the maiden':

> Come, all ye jolly ploughboys
> That want to mend the fau't;
> Be sure it is the maiden first
> That ye maun court and daut; [make much of, caress]

> For if you court the servant first,
> And gang the maiden by,
> Ye may be sure the term for you
> Is quickly drawin' nigh.

Much that we know about nineteenth-century rural courtship derives from contemporary hand-wringing over illicit sex and strong drink. The Temperance Movement campaigned to abolish hiring fairs, which they regarded as a major reason for the drunkenness and 'uncleanness' of country folk. James Inglis, son of a minister in the Mearns, claimed that they always ended in 'savage debauchery and unbridled lascivious drunkenness'. For example, *The Huntly Express* (19 November 1864) fulminated:

> It is really a barbarous-looking custom … [women] standing in rows for hours, exposed to the rain, listening to (and, we are sorry to say, often reciprocating) the ribald songs and indecent jests.

The Journal of Agriculture (1861) wrote in even stronger terms:

> Females from 14 to 25 years of age are obliged to take up their stance … and listen to all kinds of … obscene language. They are taken to public houses by their sweethearts … treated with ale or whisky, by which their passions become inflamed: all sense of shame and decency are soon lost.

John Kerr, a schools inspector who worked for many years in the Aberdeen and Banff area, was more sympathetic towards the farmworkers' need for some relief:

> I was painfully struck by the surroundings among which their lives were spent. …. The married farm-servant is usually a model of conjugal fidelity and self-denial. Tipsiness at a feeing market is no proof of much whisky being drunk or much money spent …. Scarcely tasting spirits for six months, [a] very little affects them …. It is a little hard to grudge a man whose whole life is one of unremitting toil the leaven of a holiday.

In the 1850s, for the first time, the Registrar General published the statistics for illegitimacy in Scotland. These proved to be far higher than in England, and were believed – though falsely – to be the highest in Europe. Public horror was vastly increased when the Registrar's figures revealed great differences between communities that were superficially similar. It was no longer possible to blame the 'social evil' on intemperance, bad housing, racial characteristics or type of religion, because for every example that upheld one argument there was another to disprove it. Ministers from competing Christian sects were those most confounded. 'A teenage girl in Banff was more than 20 times as likely to have a bastard as one in Ross.'

In Burns' poem 'The Cotter's Saturday Night' the dawn of young love is followed by a decorous meeting between parents and their daughter's bashful wooer. Despite the known facts of the poet's life such myths were swallowed as the whole truth and the only truth by middle-class Victorians eager to believe that rural courting mimicked the standards of purity imposed on their own womenfolk. Probably it often did, but those that burrowed deeper found an alternative version. In the 1870s Dr J M Strachan, a general practitioner in Dollar, wrote a series of articles for *The Scotsman* which confirmed courting habits described in the bothy ballads. Rural workers did their wooing mostly after dark, behind a haystack, in a barn, or frequently in the girl's bedroom. Young couples would remain alone together for several hours. 'The upper classes would be astonished if they knew how long such visits were continued without a fall from virtue,' Dr Strachan reassured his readers, but rather spoiled the effect by remarking elsewhere:

> Working men will not believe that it is possible to court a wife without stolen interviews with the lady sitting on the gentleman's knee … and they are totally incapable of conceiving that a kind look or a gentle pressure of the hand will yield delight a thousand times more exquisite than the coarse feelings in which they themselves indulge.

The present writer's grandmother did her courting in this way in the late 1890s closeted with her future husband in the servants' lavatory of a large house in St Andrews, yet managed to go to her wedding night completely ignorant about the facts of sexual intercourse. Perhaps this does not count – the chastity of Irish Catholic girls, strictly disciplined by their priests, provided a sorrowful comparison to Kirk of Scotland moralists.

In the Highlands the young did much of their courting at the summer shielings, after they had herded the animals up to the high pastures. The women and children remained in the hills for the whole of the summer, while the men would visit them to court their sweethearts and bring down the butter and cheese. Ramsay of Ochtertyre, who writes about life there in the late eighteenth century, probably comes close to reality, if one judges by the illegitimacy rate for the Highlands. Compared with other regions it remained low until about 1900. After that it rose steadily until the 1930s, in contrast to the pattern of decline elsewhere:

> Their pastoral life, and the strain of their poetry, contribute not a little to promote love-marriages. In following their cattle during the summer season,

the young people of both sexes have opportunities of familiar undisturbed conversation, which, from their manners and climate, are seldom abused. Their song and other poetical compositions abound also with examples of disinterested love.

One wonders whether Ramsay had heard of a custom of the Highlands and Western Islands known as 'bundling'. To do their courting, a young man and woman would go to bed together, sometimes wrapped in separate blankets, sometimes with a bolster between them or with the girl stitched into a pillow case from the waist down. This was carried out with full approval and sometimes in the presence of their parents. The same custom was well known in Orkney and Shetland. After a wedding it was also common for young unmarried people to pile into the 'lang bed' together, perhaps to recoup their energies for the next stage of the long celebrations.

Where occupations were by their nature tied to specific localities, communities evolved that were tightly knit and exclusive. A collier or fisherman would almost invariably marry the daughter of a fellow-worker, a tradition that continued long after social barriers had begun to break down elsewhere in society. Both these hazardous occupations depended on the presence of a strong, independent woman to run the home. The collier's wife had to provide hot water every night, deal with the coal dust her man brought into the home, and keep his grime-stiffened clothes reasonably wearable. Fisherwomen baited the lines, mended nets and sold the produce. In both occupations it was vital that a prospective bride should know what she was taking on.

Other factors became important in social circles where there were questions of inheritance or social status to consider. By the middle of the eighteenth century, the daughter of a minor laird, 'a penniless lass wi a lang pedigree', could restore her family's fortune by marrying a banker or prosperous merchant, but prominent landed families used marriage in the same way as their ancestors always had, as a bidding card in the search for political and social advancement. A marriageable son or daughter could be the means of uniting two estates. Prominent public figures moved their families from town to country and back again, observing a social calendar that maximised their opportunities. By the nineteenth century there was a prescribed series of annual events that fitted into the London 'season'. One main purpose was to find suitable spouses for their children.

The middle classes mimicked the aristocracy as far as they could. As well as private dinners, they organised local concerts and dances, amateur theatricals and charity bazaars. In these settings, young men could respect-fully pay court and young women modestly allow admirers to press their suit. Persistence rather than passion was required. In the 1880s Dr Gunn, as a young medico in his first appointment, used to ride past frozen Lindores Loch on his daily round:

> Among the throng of skaters was one who intrigued me much. This lady, hazel-eyed with Grecian features and a complexion of magnolia blossom, would glide gracefully along the glassy surface in the frosty winter sunlight; usually alone, but sometimes with an accompanying male, whom I urgently desired to put to death …. I forthwith resolved to learn to skate …. Night after night … I secretly made my way to the shores of the loch, and there for hours … I practised … usually I chose a moonless night … as there was less fear of being discovered …. In dancing also, I now resolved to acquire skill, both in order to oust other partners from the side of my adored, and to avail myself of the opportunities for meeting her which the winter social gatherings afforded.

Their first waltz proved a disaster. Dr Gunn was determined to learn to dance gracefully. He studied the steps in his room at night and during rounds he used to tether his horse to a fence on some quiet road and practise:

> At every concert where my lady-love was expected to sing … I contrived to be present … I usually arranged to have a visit in the neighbourhood, or a convenient baby to be vaccinated. On one occasion I attended a lengthy lecture on Mohammed the Prophet solely for the purpose of escorting my fair companion home.

His determination brought him the prize. Dr Gunn and his hazel-eyed Grecian were married on 31 March 1887 and lived together for forty-three years.

This history, charming though it is, illustrates the restraints imposed on young middle-class women in the Victorian and Edwardian periods. Only those fortunate enough to be born into families both well heeled and unorthodox experienced the freedom that all contemporary women take for granted. There were of course many that threw off such restraints, but the conventions of an age are defined by the expected norm, not by those who break them.

During all historical periods society demanded that a girl of so-called

'good' family should remain chaste until marriage. The reasons were based on both religion and a hard-headed concern that property should pass to a man's own children, not someone else's. The 1800s added that peculiarly exalted sentiment woven round the virgin 'rosebud garden of girls' who mysteriously transformed into angels in the house after marriage. How this came about was seldom explained to the girls themselves; they only knew that there were clear boundaries of time and place beyond which they could not socialise with men outside their own family until an engagement was announced. The presence of a 'chaperone', a married woman who kept a watchful eye on proceedings, allowed a little more licence, but physical intimacy was unthinkable before the wedding. Most of these women must have grown up uninstructed in the details of sexual activity or reproduction.

Along with Victorian sentiment went a chivalry and attentiveness that mourners for times past will nowadays find only in a certain type of romantic fiction. Such cosseting carried its price. The middle-class male lost status unless his income was large enough to keep his wife and unmarried daughters in ostentatious idleness; and for many couples, the result was hope deferred and a long engagement.

Queen Victoria and her Prince Consort stamped themselves on public consciousness as an ideal of domestic bliss for every bride and groom. Yet this was the age in which the divided spheres of work and home reached a hitherto unparalleled state of separation. Among the middle classes, clubs and other social institutions encouraged any man who wished it, to continue his bachelor lifestyle outside the home. For many, this could include undetected sexual freedom. The angel in the house was safely chained to her pedestal, and society kept the angel's wings extended by blatantly accepting a double standard of sexual behaviour.

Before he even spoke to his future wife, Dr Gunn had pointed her out to his mother. In an earlier age that would have seemed very scant courtesy. At all levels of society, family and friends involved themselves in the choice of a spouse and their advice prevailed to a surprising degree. It seems strange to us today that even the proposal of marriage was often made by a third party. Archibald Johnston of Wariston, a prominent supporter of the Covenant, described his marriage to Jean Stewart in one of his many earnest self-examinations. He was twenty-one at the time (1632):

> Thou inclyned not to the match, for they reported schoe was but ane bairne [not yet fourteen] and not to be maryed for ane year, and then that schoe was haistie and kankard, and that hir faice was al spoiled by the poks, quhilest thou wald haive bein suddenly maryd with on that was meak and faire … the Saturday thairafter thou sau hir and consented to the proponing of the mariage, yet … having no … great lyking to it, bot indifferently submitting thyselth to Gods providence and friends counsel.

It was in this frame of mind that he reluctantly gave permission for his mother to approach Sir Lewis Stewart, who accepted her proposal.

Social pressure demanded that ministers of the Kirk should be particularly careful in their choice of a wife. This may account for the rather distasteful weighing up of pros and cons found in some clerical memoirs, where personal affection seems to be the last thing on the diarist's mind. In delightful contrast is the appreciation of his good luck expressed by Alexander ('Jupiter') Carlyle, minister of Inveresk, writing forty-odd years later about his courtship and marriage in 1760. Dr Carlyle belonged to the Moderate wing of the Kirk, and moved in high intellectual and social circles. He had previously fallen deeply in love with a woman whom he pursued for nearly twenty years, and another for seven, but neither of them wanted to marry a clergyman.

He had known Sarah and Mary Roddan since their childhood. After losing both parents as small girls, they were separated and brought up by relations in very different ranks of society. Sarah was the beauty of the two:

> Sarah, the eldest, had seemingly many advantages above her sister … and accordingly turned out an elegant and well-bred woman, speaking perfectly good English … and was admired, courted and respected wherever she went. [Mary had] an expressive and lively countenance, with a fine bloom, and hair of a dark flaxen colour … excellent parts, though uncultivated and uncommon, and a striking cheerfulness and vivacity of manner.

Dr Carlyle's friend, John Hume (author of *Douglas*), who was related to the sisters, encouraged him to become better acquainted with Mary. 'Without this support,' he says, 'I would never have attempted it, on account of the inequality of her age and mine, for she was then just past seventeen when I was thirty-eight…. After nine months' courtship … and for three months by a close though unwarlike siege, I obtained her heart and hand, and no man ever made a happier conquest'.

Dr Carlyle was inordinately proud of 'the quickness of her parts and the extent of her understanding' and of the 'open, respectful and confidential manner' in which the most brilliant figures of the Scottish Enlightenment conversed with his young wife.

John Hume lent them his house for the wedding, and Carlyle was amused to receive a visit the following day from the lawyer, Henry Erskine, and Lord Chesterhall. Erskine was in hot pursuit of Chesterhall's daughter, who coincidentally was also twenty years younger than her would-be bridegroom:

> I guessed that the real motive of this visit, as my friend [Lord Chesterhall] seldom did anything without a reason, was to see how such an unequal couple would look on the day after their marriage.

Our ancestors had no difficulty in acknowledging the importance of money. Marriage notices in eighteenth-century newspapers often carried a frank assessment of the bride's financial assets alongside her physical appearance. Even earlier, a friend remarked to Alexander Hume, when his eye fell on the Lord Justice Clerk's pretty daughter: 'Faith, Sandy, you are a good marksman. She is the best fortune in Scotland.'

Adult children were grateful for their parents' meddling. A responsible father would look for a son-in-law whose family could enhance his daughter's social status, but not at the price of squandering her tocher [dowry]. In the case of a son, a judicious marriage could set him up for life. Old family land and the liquid assets of burgh merchants had a natural attraction for each other and their interaction was frequently mediated through marriage. By the late seventeenth century most burgesses would be related through blood or marriage to some local laird, and vice versa. The landed and legal classes became identified with each other in the same way, although there the coinage was the latter's expertise in court procedure.

Very few, however high their rank, could afford to ignore material advantage. How much choice of partner the parents allowed their children would depend on the relationship between them. Sir John Clerk of Penicuik wrote in *Memoirs of My Life*:

> I was about 24 years of age [the date was 1700] when I was admitted an Advocat, and a little after my Father tried all the ways he could think of to have me marry with some prospect of real advantage to my Fortune. He had projected a Wife for me … but the Lady was not to my taste …. The next attempt my Father made was for the daughter of a certain Lord, afterwards an Earle, but before I made any advances that way, I found she was engaged to a neighbouring Gentleman …. The third attempt of this kind was indeed a choise of my own, Lady Margaret Stuart, the eldest sister of the Earl of Galloway …. We contracted a friendship and familiarity with one another in the space of 5 or 6 months …. My Father was exceedingly pleased with the match.

Occasional clashes were inevitable. John Ramsay of Ochtertyre remained a bachelor himself, but took a keen interest in his neighbours' marriage plans. He frequently gossips about them in his letters. To one friend he wrote that a woman he knew 'beat her daughter black and blue' because she refused to accept the husband chosen for her. He adds almost gleefully that the girl has run off with her lover.

One of Ramsay's tenants was also having problems – his daughter had fallen in love with a man whom the farmer intensely disliked. The family was at loggerheads, and the girl threatening to elope. Then her grandfather intervened (27 July 1802):

> 'James, put her off like an honest man's daughter: lambs' flesh and lasses flesh will not take salt. As well may one think of herding a parkful of maulkins [hares] as a lass that has set her heart on a man.'

Nevertheless, like most people of his period, Ramsay strongly disapproved of unsuitable marriages. 'Unsuitable' covered any great disparity in rank, family connections, income or religion. He writes scathingly about 'a bachellor of good standing' who has made himself the 'spech of the country' by proposing to marry his housekeeper, who was also his cousin.

Captain Burt, who was stationed in Scotland between the '15 and '45 Jacobite Risings, thought that Scotsmen placed great importance on a woman's breeding potential:

> The Men have more Regard to the Comeliness of their posterity, than in those countries where a large Fortune serves to soften the hardest Features ... their Definition of a fine Woman seems chiefly to be directed to that purpose; for, after speaking of her Face, they say, 'She's a fine, healthy, straight, strong, strapping Lassie'.

Whether someone was successful in the search for a marriage partner did not depend on mutual liking alone. On top of economic necessity is the unchanging fact that the Scottish population has always contained more women than men. Over the country as a whole in the 1790s they outnumbered them by an average of one hundred to ninety. In areas such as the Highlands, emigration and army recruitment policy increased the imbalance. Through the 1800s up to 1931 these percentages did not greatly alter. Put another way, in the 1790s the number of unmarried women over forty-five in different parts of the country ranged from four per cent to forty per cent; and from 1860-1931, twenty per cent or more of Scots-women over fifty were unmarried. Surprisingly, despite their greater choice, the corresponding figure for men is fourteen per cent.

4
'A Marriage has been arranged ... '

Ask any group of people what they associate with the word 'engagement', and almost all will come up with 'choosing the ring together', 'congratulations', 'party' and 'presents'. The ritual surrounding a modern betrothal is largely unspoken, but its pressures are still as strong as when they were upheld by guides to social etiquette. There is a tacit understanding that events must happen in a certain way and in a certain order. Young couples who become engaged may be astonished at the transformation in their relationship when they make it public.

In *Rites of Marrying*, an examination of the modern wedding industry in Scotland, S R Charsley describes the painful embarrassment of a young woman called June who did not follow the correct procedure. Her friends all knew about her relationship, but she made the mistake of not telling them in advance that she and her fiancé had decided to become engaged and were about to go up town to look for the ring. After buying the ring 'secretly', June did not know what to do next; she was afraid to wear it and unable to deal with her friends' inquisitive probing. When she found the courage to put the ring on her finger, she wore it

The engagement picture of
Barbara Brodie and William Shewan. (SLA)

upside down until forced to admit the truth. June then had to soothe her friends' hurt feelings before the rejoicing could begin.

The joint search for an engagement ring is comparatively modern and would be very unusual before World War II. Charsley cites another example where a young man became a laughing stock to his friends because he bought the engagement ring himself and impetuously presented it to his girlfriend. Fifty or more years ago, in the same situation, his grandmother would have been flattered. Lovers have exchanged rings for centuries, both as a token of their affection and to mark a betrothal. In fact, this predates their use as a symbol of marriage. Earlier betrothal rings were usually made of silver or copper and ornamented with two clasped hands. They are known as 'fede' rings. Some are so large they must have been worn by men. James VI had a gold one decorated with an additional five diamonds, known as 'the espousall ring of Denmark'. James went to Denmark himself to bring home his royal bride, and the storms that threatened their homeward voyage sparked off the first great Scottish witch hunt. In the later Middle Ages, the love token or betrothal rings were often of gold, and jewelled. By 1600 the individual gemstones, or a cluster of them, were shaped into the form of a heart, often surmounted with a crown. When the rings carried a motto engraved inside, they were known as posy (poesy) rings. They could be either plain or studded with gemstones.

Plain gold wedding rings were certainly in use from an early period, but neither they nor the jewelled engagement ring became standard until the nineteenth century, at a time when marriage customs were acquiring their modern form. Even then, not everyone expected an engagement ring. In the fishing communities of the East Coast, they were exceptional until the late 1920s.

Thomas Somerville, father-in-law of the more famous Mary, tells us that in the later eighteenth century:

> Many young ladies carried snuff-boxes. The habit prevailed so generally, that it was not uncommon for lovers to present their sweethearts with snuff-boxes, which were to be purchased for that purpose, adorned with devices emblematic of love and constancy.

There were other kinds of betrothal gifts. In central Banffshire the bride-to-be made her man a 'waddin sark'. He in turn paid for her wedding dress. The custom was apparently still in force until the 1920s. A broken silver sixpence was more romantic, but the instances we hear about indicate hopeful young love, rather than an imminent marriage.

In Skye, according to someone who recorded her memories in 1985, the betrothal present had once been a 'cuach-phòsda', a quaich carved out of local wood. No doubt the rarity of this material (as commented on by Dr Samuel Johnson) added to the value of the gift!

Silver betrothal or 'fede' ring from the late fifteenth century, showing the common hand-in-hand device.

The most distinctive Scottish love or betrothal tokens are the heart-shaped Luckenbooth brooches that are still produced by modern jewellers. The heart motif clearly has some connection with the sixteenth-century heart ring, whose decoration is similar to the crowned heart on the Douglas coat of arms. These brooches were rarely more than two inches long and usually made of silver. Occasionally the material might be gold, and they were sometimes adorned with garnets and coloured glass. The brooches took their name from the locked booths of the jewellers who made them in the Royal Mile of Edinburgh. Similar ornaments were popular in fourteenth-century France, and there are early references to them in Scotland, such as the 'hert of gold anamelit [enamelled]' mentioned in the Treasurer's accounts for 1503. However, none of the examples that survive can safely be dated much before 1700.

Two silver Luckenbooth brooches of simple crowned heart style, inscribed 'Love me ever els never. I&M' (above) and 'Let me and th[ee] most happy be' (below).

The brooches are often in the shape of two hearts entwined with initials and a date on the reverse. There is a tradition that the brooch was used to fasten the shawl of a first baby at the christening. Nursing mothers are said to have worn them under their clothes on the left thigh as a charm against their milk drying up.

Not all engagements lead to marriage. We think of Robert Burns plighting his troth with Highland Mary over running water, and the Orcadian habit of engagement after four or five days of intense contact must surely have been regretted and retracted in some cases at least, despite George Low's claim that 'the person who dared to break the engagement made here was counted infamous, and excluded all society'. He was writing in 1774:

> There was a custom among the lower class of people in this country which has entirely subsided within these twenty or thirty years. Upon the first day of every new year the common people ... met at the Kirk of Stainhouse, each person having provision for four or five days; they continued there for the dancing and feasting in the kirk ... which seldom failed in making four or five marriages every year.... The parties agreed stole from the rest of their companions and went to the Temple of the Moon, where the woman ... prayed the god Wodden ... that he would enable her to perform all the promises ... she was ... to make to the young man present, after which they went to the Temple of the Sun, where the man prayed in like manner before the woman, then they repaired to [another] stone ... and they took hold of each other's right hand through the hole, and there swore to be constant and faithful to each other.

In former centuries the act of engagement was integrated into a marriage contract. There might be an unofficial understanding between a young man and woman if their parents approved, but the modern concept of two separate stages in a relationship did not exist. Putting an engagement notice in the papers is also a modern fashion – formerly there was only the announcement that the marriage had taken place, and it was considered rather pretentious to insert it unless the family was above a certain social level. Ramsay of Ochtertyre observed to a friend in 1807, 'I am diverted to see the weddings of our ordinary tenants' daughters inserted in ample form in the news papers'.

Even for men and women in modest circumstances it was important to define the legal position in case one of the partners died early during their marriage. Life expectancy for both sexes was low compared with that of today, and the hazards of childbirth cancelled out the fact that women usually live longer than men. Many a husband found himself a widower after only a few years of marriage.

The contract covered three main points: the timing of the marriage, the woman's tocher or dowry, and the jointure that the bride's father agreed to settle on the couple. In all three points, as with other matters concerning marriage, Scots law modelled itself closely on ancient Rome. The actual date might be left blank. If a length of time was stipulated, it was usually forty days. The legal document was drawn up by a notary.

Captain Burt reported to a friend in England:

> Now the portion or Toker, as they call it, of a Laird's eldest Daughter is looked upon to be a handsome One if it amounts to one thousand merks, which is 55l. 11s. 1½d. Sterling; and Ten thousand Merks, or 555l. 11s. 1½d. is generally esteemed no bad Toker for a Daughter of the lower Rank of Quality.

For comparison, Sir John Clerk (whose father was 'exceedingly pleased' with his choice of partner in 1700) allowed the couple 4,000 merks 'for our support during his life' and the same for his daughter-in-law's jointure. Clerk considered this 'very small things for a Lady of Quality to live on'.

The Duke of Hamilton gave his two younger daughters, Susan and Margaret, a tocher of £20,000 (Scots) each when they married in 1684 and 1686. A Scots pound was worth one twelfth of a pound sterling at this time.

The husband received his wife's tocher after the wedding, sometimes in instalments, on condition that he would return it if she died within a year and a day. If they both survived he divided an equivalent sum between any daughters born of the marriage, so that each of them would have her own tocher. The jointure was a piece of land or property yielding an annual income. If the husband died first the jointure would support his widow.

Another form of contract was a statement signed before the Session Clerk of the church where the couple were to be married. He charged them a fixed amount as a guarantee that both parties would fulfil the contract and entered their names in his register. This was called 'laying doon the pawns'. If one or the other failed to honour their promise, the money went to the injured party. It was obligatory for the banns to be called three times before the marriage could be celebrated (see p 11). The cost of the 'crying' was fixed at 7s 6d [37 p] for three separate Sundays, 10s 6d [51 p] for two, and one guinea [110 p] if the banns were called three times on one Sunday.

In legal terms a married woman passed from the guardianship of her father to that of her husband. All her moveable goods, including income, then belonged to the man she had married, and she had to accept his guidance in administering her heritable property. These stringent laws

Wedding banns, 1911. (SLA)

gradually disappeared from the late nineteenth century onwards.

It is a curious fact that solicitors now advise young couples to draw up a modern version of the marriage contract to cover the eventuality of separation. This is after a long period when marriage contracts were highly unusual except between couples with large amounts of money or property to dispose of. In its original form, the contract acknowledged that marriage affected women's lives much more profoundly than men's. Even before they bore their children, social and legal constraints forced most women to give up paid employment as soon as they married. Just before World War 1, apart from the notorious exception of Dundee, only five per cent of married Scotswomen worked outside the home compared with ten per cent in England.

In compensation for taking away her right to paid employment, society rewarded the married woman with a higher status than her single sisters and a greater freedom of movement. For middle-class women in particular, right up to the late nineteenth century, marriage was the only route of escape from a lifelong childhood in the family home.

In the Highlands and Islands there was a ceremony known as the *réiteach*, in which the bridegroom and his friends requested the bride's hand from her father and the two sides bargained over her portion. There is a memorable description of a *réiteach* in Compton MacKenzie's *Whisky Galore*.

Ramsay of Ochtertyre and Rev. John Lane Buchanan both describe the *réiteach* as a formal conclusion to something already agreed. Ramsay draws on the folk memory of his contemporaries (early nineteenth century) and his details suggest a tradition dating from an era when the bargaining was in earnest:

> The marriage contracts of the Highlanders were settled in a singular manner. The men of both families assembled, attended by a number of their friends, and the chieftain or landlord was commonly present to do honour to his dependants. While it was the custom to go armed on all occasions, they sometimes

went to the place of meeting in a sort of military parade, with pipers playing before them. A hill or rising ground was always chosen for this purpose, generally halfway between the parties. As soon as the bridegroom and his retinue appeared, an embassy was dispatched to them … demanding to know … whether they meant peace or war.

Ramsay adds that the two parties communicated through messengers until the affair was settled. Buchanan, though writing earlier in 1782, is describing events he has witnessed for himself. He is rather satirical about the way the bridegroom's friends make a set speech in his praise and tell the future father-in-law how lucky he is to receive such a proposal:

Mr and Mrs Adams request the pleasure of

Miss M. Adams

company at the marriage of their daughter, Helen Ann, to Ogilvie Mackie Hendry, at Newdownie, on Friday, 27th June, at 8 p.m.

Newdownie,
Nr. Carnoustie.   *An early reply will oblige.*

A written invitation to a wedding, early 1900s. (SLA)

> They hoped, therefore, that they [the bride's family] would make an offer of such a portion to the young woman, as might do honour to themselves and [be] worthy of so promising a young man.
>
> The portion was formerly paid in cows, sheep and goats … and this old practice is continued in full force. Even if the parents should have none, they must name a number of cows … otherwise the young man would think his dignity suffered in the eyes of his neighbours. Twenty cows are among the most moderate portions promised …. But as their cows are but few … they must take … a kind of representative value of it. Accordingly I was told a year old cow stood for one; three ewes for another; a spinning wheel for a third; two blankets for a fourth … and so on until the number agreed on was completed.

Once a settlement was reached, everyone was invited to an 'entertainment' – *ie* a meal accompanied by music and storytelling, and sometimes dancing. The bride then appeared for the first time, 'for before agreement it would have been reckoned indecent, and even ominous, to have seen her', and the bridegroom spent the night in his father-in-law's house.

The substitution of household objects for cows illustrates the way that society uses symbolism to keep ancient customs alive. The *réiteach* survived into the twentieth century, becoming ever more elaborately fictional as its original purpose fell out of kilter with modern conditions. In the Loch

Ness area, the bridegroom's party pretended to be strangers needing a bed for the night, and a considerable time would elapse before anyone brought up the true purpose of the visit.

Some elderly people recorded their memories of the *réiteach* for the School of Scottish Studies at the University of Edinburgh in the 1970s. In their accounts, which relate to the far North-West and the Hebrides, the bride herself becomes involved in the charade. The bridegroom went along with his spokesman on a prearranged night to her parents' house. After a friendly drink of whisky the spokesman asked the bride's father for some object such as a jug, an oar, a roof beam, or a boat, or offered to give a good home to a ewe lamb that was inclined to stray.

Both sides would ingeniously pursue this metaphor until imagination ran out. The bride was then allowed to enter the room. She drank out of the same glass as the groom, and the party went on all night. In some places the joking became quite rough – the father's friends would drag in one woman after another, asking whether this was the right one and dismissing each with a critical remark – too fat, too thin, too ugly, unable to milk a cow, *etc* – until they brought in the bride.

In the fishing villages near Aberdeen something similar happened. The bridegroom's father would visit the bride's parents to ask for her hand and fix a night when the young couple and both sets of parents could make final arrangements. This was the 'nicht o' the greeance' or the 'beukin nicht'.

Nowadays weddings have to be planned months in advance, especially if the reception is to be held at some popular venue. This is a recent development – increasing prosperity has made people aspire to settings they cannot provide for themselves. Previous generations would usually hold the feast at home or out of doors. Otherwise a modest spread in the Town Hall or a local restaurant was as much as most people expected. The wedding would normally follow soon after the contract was signed.

In the short time between betrothal and wedding, there were several tasks to perform. The bride's 'providing' or 'plenishing' for her new home would have been in the making since her teens. Arrangements differed in various parts of Scotland, but usually the groom's family supplied the furniture, while the bride provided the china, bedding, and linen. In country districts until the early nineteenth century, she would have spun the flax and wool herself. She stored her plenishing in a chest of drawers or plain wooden kist (box) which she sent to the new home a few days before the

Very much a family affair. In this 1910 Aberdeenshire wedding the happy couple are surrounded by three generations in their Sunday best. (SLA)

wedding. In the North-East it was considered important to leave the kist unlocked and unbound during the journey, to ensure easy childbirth.

In the East Neuk of Fife, the best maid (chief bridesmaid) had the responsibility of unpacking the plenishing and putting it away in the new home. Once the plenishing arrived it was considered unlucky for the bride to see the house before her wedding.

Women friends and relatives helped the best maid make the house ready, and in the process would play some tricks with the bed which would not be discovered until the wedding night.

High spirits and a sense of mischief are the cause of many bizarre activities immediately before the actual wedding or at crucial moments of the ritual. Tricks are accepted with good humour – but only those closest to the bride and groom are privileged to carry them out. Ultimately they spring from our fear of bad luck – by humiliating the victims, their friends ensure the demons of ill fortune will hunt elsewhere for their prey.

The same superstition prompted the soldiers who shouted obscenities at generals parading in triumph through the streets of ancient Rome.

In North-East fishing communities, invitations to the wedding were issued by word of mouth:

> Of an evening shortly before the marriage day ... the bride and bridegroom set out in company ... to invite the guests. The bridegroom carries a piece of chalk, and, if he finds the door of any of his friends' houses shut, he makes a cross on it with his chalk. The mark is understood as an invitation to the marriage. A common form of words ... is: 'Ye ken faht's adee the morn at twal o'clock. Come our in fess a' yir oose wi ye,' or, 'Come ane, come athegeethir.' ['You know what's going on tomorrow morning at twelve o'clock. Come over and fetch your whole house with you' .... 'Come one, come all together.'] The number of guests is usually large, ranging from forty to a ... hundred and twenty.

In rural communities, wedding parties were even larger; sometimes the whole parish was invited. Not many families could afford to feast such a multitude, so wedding presents often took the form of food and drink and help with their preparation. People from wealthier social circles were not under such constraints, but what they gave the bride and groom receives only an occasional mention. Writing about the style of dress in his youth (*circa* 1750), Ramsay of Ochtertyre says:

> But even then there was one article of extravagance: people thought nothing of laying out large sums of money for: Brussels lace. It was generally a nuptial present, being regarded as one of the appendages of wealth and fashion.

Articles on wedding etiquette and suggestions for presents began to be issued from the mid nineteenth century onwards. The 'bride's list' is an innovation of our own age. Most lists are standard; they revolve round domestic utensils and furnishings and differ only in their expectations about quality. Many department stores offer to carry a list for the convenience of the bride and her friends, but this seems to have little effect on the number of 'doublers' (duplicate presents), nor does its presence or absence reduce insecurity among wedding guests about 'getting it right'.

The list is linked to a slightly older pre-wedding ritual, the display of presents, which is usually held at the house of the bride's mother and mimics the Victorian 'At Home'. There are fixed days and hours when friends may call to view, and one or two at a time they are taken to admire and learn who has given what. They are offered refreshments and after an acceptable interval are expected to give way to other arrivals and depart.

The most important activity of all before the wedding centres on the choice of bridal gown.

A handsome wedding couple from the 1920s. Until the second half of the twentieth century the bride's gown closely followed contemporary fashion. (SLA)

5
Wedding Fashions

The image of billowing white tulle and satin is so powerful that a bride who strays too far from the ideal defines herself as trying to be 'different', rather than setting up an acceptable alternative.

Yet the tradition has a fairly recent origin – like so much else of wedding procedure it did not become the norm until the second half of the nineteenth century. The Victorians singled out some particular details and turned them into accepted procedure.

Until then, bride, groom and guests all wore fashionable garments as costly as they could afford. If the bride wore white, this would be a personal choice – in the Middle Ages the symbol of the bride's virginity was the loose hair flowing down her back. Extravagant materials, bright colours, and gemstones adorning both clothes and hair marked the medieval bride.

Detailed descriptions exist of wedding clothes worn by royalty and others of high birth from the Middle Ages onwards. The velvets, silks, brocades and satins are in rich colours and elaborately patterned or embroidered. The cost of even the plainer cloths would be beyond the means of ordinary people. A list of materials bought for Lady Elphinstone's marriage clothes in 1670 tells us that her gowns were made of black and white silk and silver tabby (watered silk). A Scots ell was slightly under a metre; since the price of the fifteen ells of tabby was £216.00 (Scots) – by far the most expensive item – this was probably used to make her wedding gown.

White became a favourite colour in the later eighteenth century, although by no means universal. The bride often wore a hat, sometimes with a small veil. The veil had appeared as early as the 1600s, but it did not become an obligatory part of bridal costume for another two hundred years. The long 'train' has always been a feature of the bridal gown, except during the brief reign of the crinoline, when it would have been impractical. One of the bridesmaids' tasks is to see that the train does not become entangled or soiled as the bride walks up the aisle.

Queen Victoria's wedding to Prince Albert in 1840 impressed the standard image on public consciousness – a virginal bride in white gown,

*These fashionable young ladies must have made quite an impact
at the wedding of the bride* (centre) *in the early 1900s.* (SLA)

enveloping veil, and not too much jewellery. Cream, ivory and parchment
were also favourite colours – plain white did not become predominant
until the 1950s. The gown always followed current fashion, but its present
iconic form has little to do with latest trends except for some extreme
examples that designers put on the catwalk when they present their
collections.

The veil was usually made of Brussels or Honiton lace, or sometimes
Irish point. It hung down the back from the top of the head where it was
attached with a wreath of fresh or artificial flowers. The Victorians liked
roses. Orange blossom, originally a French fashion, began to be popular
from the 1830s. By tradition the bride enters church with the veil covering
her face, and emerges after the marriage service with the veil thrown back.

In the Scottish Costume Society's journal for 1975, Anne Nimmo
describes an 1867 wedding veil that became a family heirloom. It cost
£60.00 and was …

a handsome creation of cream Honiton lace, six feet square with a four inch border of heart-shaped flowers of open lattice with appliqué edges and foliage; in each corner was a large floral spray, whilst the main area was diapered with small sprigs.

This veil was worn by the bride's sisters at their own weddings and then by her eldest daughter in 1889. Various daughters and nieces used it until 1954. Nowadays the bride's wedding veil is often made of plain net.

Flowers feature very early on in weddings – they were strewn before English brides and grooms as they left the church, while gilded bay and rosemary were used for decorations. The bride herself did not always carry a bouquet until the nineteenth century, the era when cut flowers and pot plants began to become prominent in the drawing room. This was the period, too, when the number of bridesmaids increased and their coloured dresses were carefully chosen to enhance the splendour of the bride. If they carried their own posies, these had to be less eye-catching than the bridal bouquet.

Where did the brides obtain their dresses? By 1850 large department stores were springing up in all major cities. Most of them had evolved from small drapery businesses, so the emphasis was on ready-made clothing. Those that went upmarket became outlets for wedding gowns in the latest fashion and offered alteration and dressmaking services.

The most exclusive stores were out of reach for the majority of brides, but there were other possibilities. Until the enormous increase in mass-produced garments after World War II, many women made their clothes at home or ordered them from a local dressmaker. Every small Scottish town used to support at least one skilled needlewoman who could produce garments to order, including wedding gowns. Her fees were not exorbitant and she would make suggestions about the material, although it was usual for customers to buy their own and ask her to make it up. The arrival of the mechanical sewing machine greatly encouraged the growth of home dressmaking. (The first Singer shop in the British Isles opened in Glasgow in 1856, although the company's products did not come into general use until much later.)

Dressmaking firms that catered for a select clientèle were well able to compete with the department stores, partly with the help of pull-out illustrations that came with the fashion journals. The earlier plates were hand-coloured and are now highly prized by collectors. The first plate to show a wedding dress appeared in the 1820s. Dressmakers relied on these visual aids to keep their customers up to date, and the most exclusive could create their own designs.

From the 1830s and probably before, there were companies that produced paper patterns for professional seamstresses. *The World of Fashion* made them available to its readers by including patterns with each issue from August 1850. Then, as now, the templates were often multi-purpose and of Byzantine complexity. In 1873 Butterick's set up its first British branch, and other companies quickly followed. The paper pattern counter still attracts large numbers of customers undeterred by the failure of hope before experience, and in every catalogue there is still a wedding section.

Although the worst horrors of the Victorian sweatshop vanished by 1900, the dressmaking firms drove their workers hard and often tyrannised over customers as well as staff. One of the best known was 'Miss Yorkston of George Street' (Edinburgh), who advertised as 'the only court dressmaker in Scotland'. The formidable Miss Yorkston ran her establishment with the help of four of her sisters, and was reputed to keep brides waiting in their petticoats until the wedding dress arrived in the nick of time by taxi.

Helen Price describes her mother's work at Miss Yorkston's between 1902 and 1914. During that time, Miss Bruce MacPherson helped to make over one hundred wedding dresses. They included the gown worn for the 'wedding of the year' in 1912, when Lady Redford's daughter married a rich widower from Glencorse at St Mary's Cathedral in Edinburgh. Her dress was white silk with black lace and had a four-yard train fastened to the shoulders. The whole ensemble was understood to have been 'made in Paris' – Miss Yorkston did not use labels. When the future Mrs Price gave in her notice because she was going to be married, Miss Yorkston expressed her strong disapproval, paid what was owed her, and said, 'I will give you a dress'. In traditional Yorkston fashion, the dress, a heavy blue silk, arrived the day before the wedding and was proudly worn on 3 September 1914.

Today, specialised wedding boutiques or catalogues have largely displaced dressmakers and department stores as sources for bridal wear. The goods on offer are essentially mass-produced, although the boutiques try their best to make the customer feel her needs are special, and the model chosen is individually made up for each bride. In earlier times it was considered unlucky to alter the wedding dress after the preliminary fitting.

Even after the tradition became firmly established, not every bride was married in a wedding dress:

Married in white, you've chosen all right
Married in blue, love ever true,
Married in brown, live out of town … [*etc*]

and other similar rhymes are proof of this, as well as all the surviving visual evidence.

When the wedding was held at home, the bride with well-to-do parents might prefer a going-away outfit or something that could be worn later as a day dress on formal occasions. Costume exhibitions prove that this choice had nothing to do with economy, since the garments are of high quality and must have cost as much as any wedding gown.

A well-dressed young bride marries Mr David Shewan in 1914. (SLA)

There was also the question of second marriages. Mrs John Sherwood wrote about the etiquette of weddings in 1884:

A widow should never be accompanied by bridesmaids or wear a veil or orange blossom at her marriage. She should at church wear a coloured silk and a bonnet …. It is proper for her to remove her first wedding ring, as the wearing of that cannot but be painful to the bridegroom.

For families on limited income it was common sense not to spend extravagantly on a garment that would be worn only once. The bride's wedding clothes were smarter than usual and intended for 'Sunday best'. Among the fisherfolk of Fife, it was a custom until the 1920s for the groom's family to take their future daughter-in-law to Dundee or Edinburgh and pay for her wedding outfit. Her in-laws had even bought her corsets, one gratified

This wedding picture from Shetland in 1919 shows an unusual choice of dress. (SLA)

wife reported. The groom's suit was tailored – he too would later wear it on Sundays.

A fashion which has completely died out at weddings is the habit of giving some item of clothing as 'favours' to the wedding guests. The gifts consisted of gloves, scarves, garters and ribbons, and were either worn at the wedding or sent round to the guests afterwards. In Scotland the minister was given a hat as well. George Ridpath notes in his diary for 20 October 1759, 'It is droll that the bride or bridegroom have sent no gloves'. He received them when the bride's parents returned home:

> Sunday November 4th .... Preached on Jeremiah 9. 23, 24. Had my marriage trophies on, hat and gloves.

In pictures of nineteenth-century weddings the bridegroom and male guests often wear a knotted white ribbon on one arm. The favour worn on the man's coat or smock was originally a ribbon rosette which changed to a floral buttonhole from the mid-century onwards. This is the origin of the extra buttonhole stitched into the left lapel of a man's jacket.

Although the status of the bride demands that she make a once-in-a-lifetime effort for her special day, it is now acceptable for a man to display himself in borrowed clothing. The male fashion of plain dress or frock coats for weddings began in the Victorian age. The helpful Mrs Sherwood again:

> No man ever puts on a dress coat before his 7 o'clock dinner, therefore every bridegroom is dressed in a frock coat and light trousers of any pattern.

In earlier ages, bridegrooms were as conspicuous as their brides for gorgeous apparel. Ramsay of Ochtertyre tells us:

> [Before the 1745 Rising] it was the etiquette, not only when they married, but also when paying their addresses, to get laced clothes and laced saddle furniture – an expense which neither suited their ordinary appearance nor their estates. No people went formerly deeper into that folly than the Highland gentry when they came to the low country.

One of the most fascinating aspects of Scottish wedding fashion is the emergence of the kilt and all its accoutrements. After the '45, wearing Highland dress was a punishable offence except for Scottish army regiments and women. The ban was not lifted until 1783. It must have

The wedding of Duncan Michie to Susan Stuart in 1937, at which the young men seem to be very proud to wear kilted attire. (SLA)

been hard to enforce in remote areas, and the existence of so many paintings executed between the two dates that show figures wearing the forbidden garments proves that it was widely disregarded by gentry and common folk alike. After 1783 there began a self-conscious revival among social groups that would have abhorred the association before Prince Charlie's Jacobite adventure.

The first active promotion of Highland dress as such coincided with the Napoleonic Wars, chiming in with the fad for imitating military uniforms. With the publication of Walter Scott's *Lady of the Lake* in 1810, the Scottish tourist industry took off in earnest. Awareness spread across the Channel when the Highland regiments marched into Paris after Waterloo. Their appearance aroused excited comment (including what must be the original version of 'What does the Scotsman wear under his kilt?') and tartan became fashionable wear.

However, it must be remembered that 'tartan' and 'Highland dress' are not synonymous. Chequered material (the original definition of 'tartan') was popular in the Lowlands – a length of it draped into a plaid was worn by Border shepherds as the most convenient form of outdoor garment, while eighteenth-century Scotswomen almost universally wore a tartan cloak also termed a 'plaid', which evolved into the shawl that female workers wrapped around themselves until late in the 1800s.

Sir Walter Scott is not entirely to blame for the nineteenth century flood of bogus tartans – the Highland Society of London was pestering clan chieftains for their non-existent setts (patterns) from 1815 – but King George IV's 1822 visit to Edinburgh, organised by Scott, certainly began the process that now identifies the whole of Scotland with its most spectacular and depopulated region. In his role as master of ceremonies, Scott was responsible for transforming an outmoded everyday garment into an elaborate form of fancy dress. Elizabeth Grant remarks about George's visit:

> A great mistake was made by the stage managers – one that offended all southron Scots; the King wore at the levée the Highland dress. I daresay he … did not know the difference between the Saxon and the Celt.

It is debatable how far the kilt – either as belted plaid or truncated *fileadh beg* – ever came back as ordinary wear for the majority of Highlanders after 1783. Contemporary accounts give a conflicting impression. Most suggest that the kilt was confined to what the writers described as 'the lower orders'. Elizabeth Spence, in 1816, looked out for signs of what Thomas Pennant had described fifty years earlier in *A Tour in Scotland,* and concluded:

> Our English habit begins now to be substituted … for their own national attire … the elderly men use the Scotch bonnet universally, and are always habited in a suit of light blue cloath, which materials are wove at home. They enwrap themselves in the drapery of the plaid.

Captain Burt had already noted before the '45 that Highland gentlemen wore 'trowse' [trews] with a plaid, 'and the whole garb is made of chequered tartan', while the belted plaid was 'the common habit of the ordinary Highlanders'.

Genuine Highland dress does appear in the 1820 wedding described

This rather stately affair, in 1937, is the wedding of the Marquis of Douglas and Clydesdale and Lady Elizabeth Percy, with the groom wearing Highland regalia to full effect. (SLA)

below, but only half the men are wearing it. Perhaps it was already being kept for high days and holidays. The excerpt is from the *Inverness Courier*:

> Last week a wedding was solemnized in the wild but beautiful Glen of Urquhart … betwixt George Anderson, the blacksmith of the district, and Marjorie May Macdonald, a decent young damsel, who belonged to the same parish …. There were in all four hundred persons assembled. All the maidens displayed their snoods and plaids, about ninety of the young men were dressed in full Highland garb.

The next impetus given to this trend came through the institution of Highland Games and the example set by Balmoral. All male members of the royal family put on Highland dress on their summer visits to Queen

63

Victoria's 'dear Paradise'. In imitation, the owners of sporting estates began to clothe their gillies in tartan and themselves assumed the kilt with all its expensive extras. Four of Victoria's sons wore Highland dress at their sister's wedding in 1858 when the Archbishop of Canterbury married the Princess Royal to the Crown Prince of Prussia in St James's Chapel, London. We can assume the middle orders caught the habit from their betters.

The modern kilt, with its stiff military pleating and jackets for every occasion, is the product of this artificial revival, but worn only on special occasions such as weddings, ceilidhs and football internationals. In both Highlands and Lowlands only those determined to make a point use it as everyday wear.

Late nineteenth-century photos show the kilt being worn at funerals rather than weddings. As a costume for children, 'Highland' kilts and jackets came into vogue quite early, possibly through the fashion for putting them into fancy dress that arose in the late eighteenth century along with the development of more natural juvenile clothing. The 1840s album of photos by Adamson and Hill show boys well under ten kitted out in kilt, jacket and sporran – the large hairy variety drooping to the knees that was favoured in the reign of Victoria.

Even earlier, in 1794, Donald Sage describes how he and his three brothers and sisters dressed to receive their father back home for '*a' bhanais theth*' (the heating of the house) after his second wedding. Mr Sage senior was the minister of Kildonan in Sutherland.

> At my father's marriage none of his children were present – we were too young. [They were all under ten years old. Donald, the youngest, was five.] …. When the happy pair arrived … we were, after a long previous drilling in the nursery, marshalled by Eppy [the housekeeper] to the kitchen door …. Both my sisters were dressed in tartan gowns of home manufacture, their hair was braided on the forehead, and saturated with pomatum, and they were made to look, upon the whole, just like two young damsels from a Highland nursery, making their first appearance in public life. My brother and I were clothed in the same identical tartan, but of a make and habit suited to our age and sex. This was a kilt after the most approved fashion, surmounted by a jacket, fitted tight to the body, and to which the kilt was affixed by a tailor's seam. The jacket and kilt, open in front, were shut in upon our persons with yellow buttons. Our extrem-ities were prominently adorned, and Eppy, who was a first-rate Highland dressmaker, had exhausted her skill upon them, and even outdone herself. We were furnished with white worsted stockings, tied below the knee with red

garters, of which 'Malvolio' himself would have approved. Our feet were inserted into Highland brogues, while our heads were combed and powdered with flour, as a substitute for the hair-powder which was the distinguishing mark of all the swells of that fashionable age.

Their stepmother received the four small Highlanders 'very graciously', and looked at the two girls with 'an arch smile':

> When we … with our kilts and jackets, and, above all, our highly-powdered heads, met her eye, she could no longer contain herself, but burst into an uncontrollable fit of laughing, in which my father, and even Eppy herself were all obliged to join.

Happily, this did not stop the children enjoying the marriage feast.

Apart from the rules applied to female competitors at Highland Games, there has been no strong revival of Highland dress for women comparable with the re-emergence of the kilt. Some sources say that it was customary for a Highland bride to wear a new plaid to her wedding. It is not so usual to find girls in Highland dress at weddings, but an 1898 photo shows the eight bridesmaids of Lady Flora Douglas-Hamilton decked in plaids and tricorn hats and holding tartan-wrapped bouquets. The bride wears a conventional wedding dress.

6
The Stag, the Hen, and
the Old Wives' Tale

'The evening before a wedding,' writes Captain Burt, 'there is a ceremony
called the feet-washing.' This custom was universal throughout Scotland
until the nineteenth century, although it sometimes took place on a
different night. Fife mining families did their 'feet-washing' immediately
after asking the minister to proclaim the 'cries' or marriage banns. At
some point in the 1800s, feet-washing began to merge with the general
pre-wedding celebrations.

As a distinctive ritual it was remarkably consistent in every region of
the country. Friends and relations would go to the respective homes of the
bride and groom to wash their feet in a tub of water. The ceremony was
loud and chaotic, because everyone had to take a turn at the washing. The
guests amused themselves with singing and dancing, while large quantities
of food and drink encouraged their efforts. Orcadians filled the tub with
mingled salt and fresh water, and in Shetland, if the family was wealthy
enough, the bridegroom's feet were washed in wine.

In Orkney it had once been a solemn occasion – the bride's father took off
her shoes and her mother spoke a blessing as she removed the stockings.
This suggests that the custom originated in a ritual purification similar to
the Scandinavian 'bride's bath'. Thomas Newte, in his *Observations* of 1791,
compares it to a similar Persian custom where the guests used henna to
stain the bride's hands and feet and painted her eyebrows with antimony.
Henna and water figured in ancient purification rites in the Middle East,
and according to Chambers's *Book of Days* Armenian brides were still
tinted in the same way in 1869. The same wedding customs exist in the
Middle East today.

The attendants of a Scottish bride threw various small objects into the
washing tub, the most important of which was a ring – either the actual
wedding ring borrowed from the groom, or one lent by a married woman.
There was a damp and noisy struggle as everyone competed to fish it out
of the water. The winner would be the next to marry.

In the Inverness district the ritual was known as *'glanadh nan cas'*. The bridegroom's friends smeared his feet and legs with soot, supposed to have magic powers because of their connection with the hearth and fire:

> At the same time as the process of washing the feet went on, efforts were persistently made to blacken them with soot. Sometimes the legs, and even the face, came in for a rubbing, and thus, washing and blackening alternated, until, after a while, the fun was discontinued, and music and dancing were indulged in, and kept up until an early hour.

In 1811, sixteen-year-old Harriet Westbrook and her groom eloped from England to Edinburgh, where their landlord paid for the wedding on condition that he and his friends were invited to the supper. After the couple finally managed to retire to their bedroom, the landlord knocked on the door and announced, 'It is customary here at weddings for the guests to come in, in the middle of the night, and wash the bride with whisky'. It is not clear whether this attempt to combine feet-washing with the bedding of the bride was a local peculiarity or the result of the refreshments served. In any case, the intruder rushed away at top speed when the furious groom whipped out a pair of duelling pistols and threatened to blow out his brains. The groom's name was Percy Bysshe Shelley.

John Dixon, writing about the remote North-West, claimed that in the Gairloch district feet-washing was 'strictly observed to the present day' (*ie* 1886), but elsewhere by then the custom seems largely to have died out in its original form. Even when the name lived on, the feet-washing was often a spontaneous affair and an excuse for what southern Scots called 'the blacking' or 'blackening'. In some areas only the bridegroom was blackened – where the bride received the same treatment she was usually left to the untender mercies of her women friends.

Taped accounts in the School of Scottish Studies suggest the ritual washing was eventually reduced to a necessary part of clearing up the mess. The fun lay in causing the victim as much discomfort as possible. Bridegrooms were grabbed when they were least expecting it and smeared with shoe polish or even stickier substances. The blackening could extend beyond the feet to more intimate parts of the body as the tormentors wrenched off the groom's clothes or ruined them in the scuffle. Female relations often took part – the sexual horseplay recorded sounds very like the bacchanalian reactions to modern male strippers.

In the years after World War II there were three essentials for a really good feet-washing: events must erupt like a thunderclap, the groom must protest and struggle before submitting, and both he and all washable surfaces (ideally, newly cleaned) must end up smeared with cocoa, treacle, or shoe polish – anything the kitchen provided. Then for years to come his mother, sisters and aunties could gleefully recall their night of pandemonium.

Nowadays the last day at work before the wedding still ends with some kind of licensed foolery. The extremity of tricks played depends very much on the nature of the victims' workplace and whether it employs both men and women. For a groom alone with male colleagues the joking can border on violence; if the workforce is mixed there is usually more restraint. Men-only celebrations traditionally culminate in a stag night at some hotel or public house where the aim is to test the groom's manhood by making him as drunk as possible and then leave him chained to a lamppost in the minimum of clothing.

Yet the wind of change is blowing through these rough pastures. The workplace is increasingly a mixed environment, and pre-wedding celebrations are changing to suit new conditions. Even in the late 1980s, when Charsley made his study of Scottish wedding traditions, some brides expressed irritation at the artificial division between the sexes on this one particular night. International company offices with their streamlined ranks of computers are not as indulgent to fooling around as the old factory or shop floor. When the groom's friends insist on a stag night, it does not always conform to the stereotype. In England the adventure playgrounds advertised in men's magazines are a popular alternative for giving the groom a last fling with the lads. Will the trend spread northwards? Managers of upmarket Scottish restaurants report that when the stags canter into their premises they try to give the groom a good time rather than humiliate him. Worse still for diehards who love their ancient stamping grounds, the hens are beginning to join in.

In the factory towns of Central Scotland the feet-washing of the bride developed into a rowdy event known as 'jumping the chanty' on the night of the 'pay-off'. On the last day of work the woman's friends would dress her up in fantastic garments that parodied the bridal finery she would wear to her wedding. Details varied, but typically they would deck her in lace curtains covered with paper flowers and present her with a vegetable bouquet. The central feature was a 'chanty' or chamberpot filled with salt which she had to carry while her friends walked or barrowed her round the workplace for colleagues to wish her luck, kiss her, and push a silver coin into the salt. When the money was counted, no one could identify the donors or their size of contribution. The salt contained lucky items connected with pregnancy and motherhood, as well as slips of paper on which the bride's friends had scribbled bawdy rhymes about the wedding night.

The workplace celebrations ended with the bride 'jumping the chanty' three times to cheers and shouts from her audience. Then her friends paraded her through the busiest streets of the town extracting money from the men they met and inviting them to kiss the bride. This was done not too unwillingly, especially by the older men who were reported to be the most generous. (One cynic claimed they were seizing a rare opportunity to kiss a pretty girl.)

A striking aspect of Scottish wedding customs is the ability to survive by adjusting to the conditions of city life. Scots have favoured tenement living since the medieval period, and many still do (what else are Edinburgh's New Town and Glasgow's Merchant City except glorified tenements?), but it was not until the Industrial Revolution that thousands began to cram the narrow Central Belt and preserve as best they could the habits and traditions of their rural homelands. Asking money from strangers was perhaps an adaptation of the old 'penny wedding' (see p 86).

In Glasgow the bride's friends paraded her round areas where vertical living enforced a warm neighbourliness between the street and those ensconced in the eyries above it. As the bride passed, up went the tenement windows and showers of small change descended into an outspread sheet. In a recent newspaper article this is cited as a modern custom, but the window shower was already known in Edinburgh by 1842.

James McLevy, a detective with a sharp eye and a taste for appalling puns, had traced a series of house-breakings to a young hawker called Lizzy Gorman. He intended to arrest her in the very middle of her wedding in the Cowgate. The police have taken up position as McLevy prepares to move in:

'Are the constables ready?' I whispered to my assistant.
'Yes; they're in the stair-foot beyond the meal-shop on the other side.'
'Then keep your post, and have an eye to the window.'
'For *ha'pennies?*' said he with a laugh.
'I'm just afraid I may reduce the *happiness*,' replied I, not to be outdone in Irish wit on a marriage occasion.

Many of the women who described jumping the chanty belonged to a generation that thought it socially unacceptable for them to enter bars without a male escort. In those days the bride's procession made such a din outside the pub that the men came out to pay their dues to the chanty and send the women on to plague other drinkers. The pay-off would end about ten o'clock; the women went back to the bride's home for a snack supper, and, if they were lucky, their own drinking spree.

Now that women are free to drink wherever they like, the pay-off can go straight from work to pub – or several pubs – and may even start off from home after the show of presents. The procession through the streets is split into short forays from bar to bar. Those brave enough may let their friends wheel them in on a supermarket trolley. If the licensee thinks it will not annoy his other customers, the good-humoured stand-and-deliver goes on in the bar as well as the street. The evening may end at a club or disco. In these circumstances the lassies' night out becomes a female equivalent of the stag night. By the end of the evening, hens as well as stags have certainly drunk their fill.

The association of a chanty with the marriage eve goes back at least to the early 1800s. In the West of Scotland, when the chief bridesmaid escorted the 'plenishing' to the new home, she carried a chanty packed with salt which she sprinkled over the floor to guard against the evil eye. After this precaution she would rejoin her friends for the feet-washing. In the North-East the chanty full of salt was still a common wedding present in the early 1930s. Miniature versions decorated with an eye or gilding were on sale at trinket stalls in Aberdeen Market.

The use of the chanty in pre-wedding frolics springs from the same impulse that leads to the over-decoration of public conveniences. In primitive belief all bodily fluids are potential sources of magic. The salt is a substitute for the chanty's normal contents. In the Western Highlands urine was ritually sprinkled over buildings, equipment and animals to guard against the evil eye. Salt could be used as a substitute, for instance, when the animals were first driven to the fields from their winter quarters.

Modern sanitation has turned the pottery 'chanty' into a collector's prize and its weight is too heavy for a feeble race unaccustomed to the vigorous mangling and sheet-hanging of our foremothers. Where the custom is still upheld, the chanty has dwindled to a tinware basin or bowl made of plastic.

Marriage is an obvious target for the anxiety attached to any major life change. The wedding day has generated superstitions that not even the most up-to-date bride manages to throw off completely. Diverse and puzzling as they may seem, all originate from the belief that individuals are vulnerable to the power of evil spirits while they pass between old and new. Counter magic is activated through ritual, while omens can warn of coming disaster. Then one can take avoiding action. For example, the bridegroom lifts the bride over the threshold to prevent her stumbling as she enters her new home – the worst possible augury for their future. In some areas of Scotland the best man slept with the groom on his wedding eve, and the bridesmaid with the bride, to protect them against evil.

A rural population forms its superstitions round natural phenomena. While a wet wedding day is only an inconvenience for modern city-dwellers, in the past it was a bad omen for the couple's happiness. For the same reason fine weather was a cause for rejoicing. Most months were fortunate, with the strong exception of May. 'Marry in May, rue for aye', says the proverb; and, more specifically, 'O marriages in May/Bairns die in decay'. Highlanders had a particular aversion to the third of May. Pennant tells us: 'A Highlander never begins anything of consequence on the day of the week on which the 3rd of May falls, which he styles "*la seachanta na bliadhna*" – and that included marriage. Marriage rates have always dropped in May and soared in June, also a favourite wedding month for ancient Romans, since it was dedicated to Juno, the goddess of marriage and family. Like us they avoided May, because it held three festivals of mourning for the dead.

The day after Mary Stewart married the Earl of Bothwell in May 1567, a placard appeared outside Holyrood Palace inscribed with a quotation from Ovid, '*Mense malas maio nubere vulgus ait*' ['The people say that (only) unlucky women marry in May'] – and no doubt the anonymous protester was highly pleased when events justified his prophecy.

The favourite season for weddings in Orkney and Shetland was the winter, perhaps because agricultural work was then at its slackest. It also allowed betrothed couples to link their wedding with the good luck of the New Year. December 31 was the most popular choice, particularly if the wedding took place with 'the moon growing, the tide flowing'. This day was also a favourite in other parts of Scotland.

The Highlanders considered it hazardous to enter on 'straddling marriages', that is when the banns were proclaimed in one year and the wedding celebrated in the next. The same dislike applied to the 'terms' when tenants paid their rent. Conversely, the Fife miners did not like to be married by a newly-called minister (he had not proved his 'luck') – if necessary, they would even go to one of another denomination.

In Scotland generally the favourite weekday for marriage used to be Friday, although there were local variations. In Orkney and Shetland it was usually a Thursday.

Many wedding customs, such as tossing the bride's bouquet into the crowd, spring from a hope of sharing her good luck. Examples are: scrambling for the ring at the feet-washing, 'rubbing shoulders' with the bride when she becomes engaged, and putting a piece of wedding cake under the pillow. A strange instance is the misbehaviour after wedding services reported from Elgin in the seventeenth and eighteenth centuries. When the minister began his blessing, the congregation would rush out pell-mell to 'catch the blessing'. If there were several couples being married, they would compete to be the first to leave the church. The following incident happened in 1750:

> At Rathven Church … October 14. Two couples, having been married on the Thanksgiving Day, there happened a very disorderly throng in outgoing of the people by their not waiting to hear the last prayer or blessing, by running out as soon as the prayer began, Angus Cormach, taking his sister, one of the brides, out of her seat, and John Runcie [the minister] calling on the brides to go out of doors hand in hand.

Most post-wedding customs were an expression of joy that the perilous transition between old and new had been safely accomplished. Once the ceremony was over, the guests could concentrate on other matters, such as having a good time and encouraging the bride's fertility. It was an old belief that a woman would be fruitful if her marriage bed was made up by a nursing mother; similarly, the bridal procession might be led by a woman with milk in her breasts. One final attempt to scare off evil spirits was the habit of firing off guns during the processions both to and from church. This was specially characteristic of Highland weddings.

The superstitions that are observed today relate mostly to the bride's clothing and they are as ancient as others that have fallen into disuse. The blue that the well-known rhyme urges the bride to wear was usually her garter, and we shall hear more about that later. In the eighteenth century, brides and grooms in the Western Isles were careful not to wear anything tightly knotted on the way to their wedding. 'Casting knots' was one method witches used to inflict a curse on someone, and who could be sure there was not a witch's knot among those already tied? It was only after the service was over that bride and groom would fasten their clothing again.

Writing about the eighteenth-century Highlands, David Stewart of Garth states that only the bridegroom untied his 'knots':

> ... nothing to be bound on that occasion, but the one indissoluble knot, which death only can dissolve. The bride was not included in this injunction. She was supposed to be so pure and true, that infidelity on her part was not contemplated. Such were the notions and delicacy of sentiment among a people esteemed rude and uncultivated.

This interpretation is a tribute to the colonel's character but not to his knowledge of anthropology – other sources state more correctly the curse that might be inflicted was sterility or impotence. This might result from sheer malevolence, but the bride had also to guard against the jealousy of rejected suitors:

> This evil result was sought to be averted by the bride wearing a sixpence in her left shoe till she was kirked; but should the bride have made a vow to any other, and broken it, this wearing of the sixpence did not prevent the evil consequences from falling upon her first-born. Many instances were currently quoted among the people of first-born children ... having been born of such unnatural shapes and natures, that, with the sanction of the ministers and the relations, the monster birth was put to death.

In some parts of the Highlands the bridegroom as well as the bride put a piece of silver into his shoe.

The bride must not let the groom see her in her wedding finery until they meet to marry; she must put on her right shoe first and carry somewhere about her a silver sixpence. She must not look at herself in the mirror when fully dressed, and it is the worst possible luck to meet a funeral on the way to her wedding. (Meeting a sweep – very lucky – is a rare event nowadays!) If the month is June, somewhere in Scotland next Saturday morning there will be a bride doing one or all of these things.

7
The Big Day

After her mother's early death Miss Maughan ran the family home at 37 Melville Street, Edinburgh. She became a lively and popular hostess who delighted in entertaining the officers from the Castle. She confessed in her autobiography, 'I have always had a weakness for soldiers, and came through scarlet fever in a by no means modified form'.

Although she was an Episcopalian, and did not enjoy social occasions 'flooded with black coats', to help out a friend she attended a reception held during the General Assembly of the Church of Scotland in 1863. She was instantaneously attracted to the handsome young minister of Roseneath, and became Mrs J L Story at the end of October:

> My old clergyman, Dean Ramsay, married us, assisted by the two curates of St John's, Mr. Carr and Mr. Sandford, and the ceremony took place in our own drawing-room, owing to the strong objection of Mr. Story's mother to a wedding in church .... She was of the old school, and nourished strong objections to all modern innovations.

There are two interesting points here: three Episcopalian clergymen are officiating at the wedding of a Kirk of Scotland minister – what would a seventeenth-century Covenanter have thought of that? – and the fashion for church marriages is beginning to set in again.

Mrs Story's attitude is rather advanced for its time. Writing about Dumfriesshire in 1903, J L Waugh says:

> If this fine [for not marrying in church] had been zealously enacted the poor's fund would have been a large one, as it is only within the last twenty years that a marriage has been celebrated in the new Parish Church.

As we saw in Chapter 2, the early Kirk imposed heavy penalties on those who did not marry in church, although there was no legal requirement to do so. The habit of marrying at home began among the proscribed Episcopalians during the seventeenth century. When the penalties were lifted after the death of the Young Pretender, most swore allegiance to the

House of Hanover and consequently Episcopalians were soon able to erect their own places of worship.

Scottish churches did not pamper their congregations. In rural areas many of them were miserably cold and damp and were situated beside ill-maintained roads that turned to mud in bad weather. In such circumstances, the tributes of a loyal tenantry were much less attractive than a good fire and undisturbed privacy for one's chosen guests. By about 1700 better-off Presbyterian families were imitating Episcopalians and gladly paid up for the convenience of marrying at home. Those who could not afford the fine continued to marry in church or at the minister's manse.

By 1800 the Kirk's insistence on marriage in church had dwindled to a formality. During the 1800s Presbyterians from all backgrounds might decide to marry in church, at home, in the minister's manse, or in a hall hired for both wedding and reception. Owners of country houses often hosted weddings for favourite servants in their own grandiose surroundings. In small islands or fishing villages the whole community would become involved, so the number participating in the celebrations could be enormous.

Where the wedding was held depended on family and community practice. Popular perception was that Highlanders married in church and Lowlanders at home, but this is only a general truth. Folklore and personal memoir do not support such a neat division. To discover why people chose any one of the four venues mentioned requires extensive research into geographical and personal detail. Why the manse rather than the church, when the two usually stood near each other? Was it always because the manse was more comfortable than the church? What decided whether the minister came to the wedding, or the wedding went to the minister? These and other such questions are beyond the scope of this book.

What can be said is that those sections of society slow to abandon church weddings seem to have taken longer to adopt them when they returned to favour. In a city even the most run-of-the-mill church nuptials entailed a high degree of public display, and Scots are famous for cutting their over-weening neighbours down to size. Certainly, during the eighteenth, nineteenth and early twentieth centuries, Church of Scotland ministers married sufficient numbers outside church premises to establish the myth that this type of wedding was a Presbyterian tradition.

How then is it that the majority of Scots now marry in a church or their local registry office? I suggest three possible influences which helped to bring on a change that must have happened over a long period of time.

First, example. During the 1800s, Parliament removed the legal disabilities of various religious groups outside the Established Church and its quarrelsome sub-divisions. Roman Catholics, Nonconformists, and those of the Jewish faith, were all married in their own places of worship. Their buildings multiplied, and so would public awareness of church or synagogue marriages, most of them among couples living in the same streets and from the same social class as their Presbyterian neighbours. Wealth may not trickle down as politicians suppose, but social custom does.

Second, the proliferation of shops and department stores offering cheaper versions of fashionable clothing, including bridal wear. This began in the mid-nineteenth century. Within our own era we have seen an enormous growth in the wedding industry. Those that choose to wear the traditional gown naturally want a stage on which to display it and the attraction of showing it off in a church wedding is irresistible.

Third, the Church of Scotland has retreated even further from its former interference in private lives – even those with minimal religious allegiance can marry within its walls without embarrassment. A large number of those who marry in church are committed Christians, but there is no doubt that to many the ecclesiastical ceremony, like the kilt, is part of the traditional flourish.

There have been two recent updates in marriage law. As well as the Christian and Jewish religions, the law recognises those practised by the ethnic minorities of Great Britain. The only condition is that the union must be monogamous and contracted between two adults, male and female. Scotland has not followed a minority of European countries in recognising same-sex marriages, although there are churches that will administer a blessing if requested.

English marriage law has also abolished the requirement for weddings to be celebrated in church. Ingenious couples have taken advantage of the new freedom to tie the knot in the air and under the sea as well as on earth. The choice has widened in Scotland as well, but not many of us seem to hanker after such bizarre locations. An alternative to the almost universal church ceremony is one held at a country hotel or ancient family castle. Several companies advertise 'real Scottish weddings' on the Internet.

The bride, Rubeena Shankar, prepares to head off to her wedding in Edinburgh, 1995. (SLA)

They promise pipers, kilted attendants, a sumptuous banquet – and of course a hefty bill for the bride's father.

Now we must haste to the bridal. In the past, except for very grand weddings, it was usual for the whole party – bride, groom and guests – to walk to the ceremony. If the distance was too great they would ride; known as a 'riding wedding'. The procession to and from church or minister's manse developed its own traditions. In its simplest form the bridal procession was so arranged that the separate parties for bride and groom reached their destination at the same time, the bride slightly in advance. The bride was escorted by two young men, and the groom by two maidens.

In the Highlands and Islands weddings were often held late in the day after prolonged celebrations that anticipated the marriage feast. A fiddler played for the indoor guests, while the overspill danced outside to the sound of the pipes. In other parts of Scotland the guests arrived early at the bride's or groom's house and consumed a large breakfast. In the North-East it was a two-course meal of porridge with milk and sugar followed by curds and cream. The guests amused themselves by dancing until it was time to set out.

Country weddings near Perth could become very boisterous well before the marriage feast:

> Sometimes the whole parish were invited .... Many of the farmers had their wives mounted behind them, and the lads their sweethearts – The moment the bride started, all the old shoes in the house were thrown after her ... and the gridiron was rung with a thundering noise. There was a halt made at every public house on the way.

'On no account could the bride and bridegroom meet on the marriage day till they met on the bride stool,' says Walter Gregor. This is the custom observed today, but it was not always so – another intriguing question for research. In the Fife mining villages the bride and groom were 'bowered', that is, the guests held green branches above their heads as the whole bridal party walked to church with linked arms.

In Shetland and Orkney as well as Perth, the guests all set out from the bride's house. In Perth a man known as 'the Send' went ahead of the bridegroom's party to announce its approach. Before the procession set off there was often a mock seizure of the bride. The most elaborate version occurred in Shetland. The bridegroom and his men walked in single file to the bride's house, where they drew themselves up in a half circle and fired three shots:

> To them from the house came the bride and her maidens, looking very demure in white dresses, white shawls, and white beribboned caps. Their apparent shyness did not prevent them from following the bride's example and kissing every man present. They had come through the door by the left side, and their progress was sunwise until they re-entered the house by the opposite side of the door.

In both Orkney and Shetland the 'wedding walk' conformed to a set pattern that lasted until World War I. At its head was a fiddler or piper. Before the party left the house he was offered a hot oatmeal pudding made from the tail of a pig – a good antidote to the whisky he consumed! In Shetland an older married couple – 'da honest folk' – walked immediately behind him and in front of the bride and groom. Orcadian processions always crossed running water twice; and the last couple, the 'tail-sweepers', dragged behind them a broom made of heather.

In most areas of Scotland the guests presented bread and cheese and whisky to the first person they met on their way to the wedding. Sometimes they forced this 'first foot' to walk with them a mile or more. Another custom during the wedding walk was to fire off guns and pistols at random. The enthusiasm reached its peak in the Highlands:

> On these occasions the young men supplied themselves with guns and pistols, with which they kept up a constant firing. This was answered from every hamlet as they passed along, so that, with streamers flying, pipers playing, the constant firing from all sides, and the shouts of the young men, the whole had the appearance of a military array, passing, with all the noise of warfare, through a hostile country.

The original purpose of the gunfire – to frighten off evil spirits – became lost in the general hilarity, and some ministers tried to stop the habit, which often interrupted the wedding service itself. At Auchenderran in Fife, the gunners were obliged to stop their fun two hundred yards from the church, which on one occasion had been damaged by the shots.

After the wedding there have always been other events before the guests leave for the reception. At Highland weddings, the bride used to kiss all the guests when she came out of church:

> Outside, after cordial hand-shaking, refreshments were served, and the toast of the newly-wedded couple was proposed and joyfully responded to. It was not uncommon to engage then, in dancing, even … when snow lay deep on the ground.

A 1930s 'wedding walk' takes place in Orkney. (SLA)

Today the piper (if there is one) strikes up, confetti is thrown at the emerging bride and the photographer strides forward to take control. A posse of guests with camcorders will be filming as well. Recording as much of the wedding as possible has become a major part of the process.

In the not-so-distant past the interval between wedding and feast was filled by the 'roping' and the 'scramble'. The happy couple would find that the local lads had bound the church gate with rope, and to secure their exit the bridegroom had to dig into his pocket. The sum expected was a pound or two and the money was usually spent in the nearest pub.

The 'scramble', 'poor out', 'scatter', 'scour-out' or 'ba siller' was more a children's affair. Here too the bridegroom and his men were expected to do the handsome thing by scattering handfuls of copper among the expectant youngsters. The sum had to cover the price of a new ball, hence the name 'ba siller' (ball money). The demand might be made outside the house or at various places en route to the wedding. The children encouraged generosity with doggerel threats and insults:

> Poor out, ye dirty brute,
> Ye canna spare a ha'penny!

Or,

> If you don't gie's a baa
> You'll hae nae weans ava.

When wedding parties began to hire chauffeured cars, guests would roll down the windows and try to throw their largesse from the passing motorcade. This was an unwelcome development – there was a risk of serious injury when the children rushed forward to scoop up the pennies, and drivers were fearful for their gleaming paintwork. To keep everyone happy, they confiscated the 'scatter', and then threw it to the bairns on a safe patch of grass.

In Edinburgh the young extortionists hounded their victims for 'ba siller' to the very threshold of escape. As 'Colonel's bairns', Alasdair Alpin MacGregor and his brother 'were discouraged from becoming too familiar with the trades-people and their progeny':

> Father deemed it most improper … that sons of his …should be seen hanging about a tenement entry or garden-gate, waiting for the emergence of the

newly-married couple. 'Poor out! Poor out!' was the recognised exhortation on such occasions. If the best-man had not flung out a sufficient sum, the more persistent might follow the old growler [cab] bearing the couple to the station, until the exasperated bridegroom appeased them by pitching out of the window all the small change he had …. We felt reticent about disclosing the source of any small wealth thus obtained.

And now to the bride's garter. She had to surrender her 'favours' (see p 60) and her garter to the invited guests immediately after the marriage ceremony. In the early eighteenth century:

> Sir James Stewart's marriage with President Delrimple's [Dalrymple] Second Daughter brought together a number of people related to both familys …. The marrige was in the Presidents house, with as many of the relations as it would hold. The Bride's favours were all sowed on her gown from tope to bottom and round the neck and sleeves. The moment the ceremony was performed, the whole company run to her and pulled off the favours: in an instant she was stripd of all of them. The next ceremony was the garter, which the Bride-groom's man attempted to pull from her leg; but she dropt it throw her peticot on the floor. This was a white and silver ribbon which was cut in small morsals to everyone in the company. The Bride's mother came in then with a basket of favours belonging to the Bridegroom; those and the Bride's were the same with the Liverys of their familys; hers pink and white, his bleu and gold colour.

Between the wedding and the marriage feast the guests held a race on foot or horseback known as 'running the broose' ('braize', 'brace' – there are many variations). For obvious reasons this was a rural custom. If the reception as well as the wedding was held at the bride's home, she walked to some chosen spot and the contestants raced towards her. The winner kissed the bride. In one Lowland event quoted from the early twentieth century he also won the prize of a white silk handkerchief.

When the wedding took place at a considerable distance from the house providing the later festivities, the guests had much farther to travel. The race, on foot or horseback, was taken very seriously. 'At riding weddings it was the great ambition of farmers' sons to succeed in winning the *braize*, and they would even borrow racing horses for the occasion.' Explanations of the race are that it is another substitute for the capture of the bride or an announcement that the wedding has been safely completed. A bowl of brose was the prize in some areas, in others a bottle of whisky.

The race seems to have lasted until the 1820s, and there are some memorable stories about it. The *Glasgow Courier* of 16 January 1813 reports one held at Mauchline, the setting for some of Robert Burns's most famous poems. The thirteen-mile race was ridden by four men and a teenager named Jean Wyllie, who 'won the broose', and lived to the age of 102!

The rivalry between the competitors could become highly dangerous, as in this eye-witness account from George Penny:

> The bride's house was on one side of the Rumbling Bridge [in Glendevon, twenty kilometres east of Stirling] and the bridegroom's on the other, so that the company had to pass it on their way home. At this time the bridge had no ledge, and was scarcely broad enough to admit the passage of a cart; and the danger was further increased by an abrupt turn of the road, close upon the bridge. The party being a little elevated … it was truly terrifying to see the horses, even those that were double mounted, rushing across this awful chasm, which is upwards of two hundred feet in depth. There were two cripple dominies [school teachers] present, one of whom … was mounted on a strong horse, with his wife behind him. In rushing past a rival in the race, the wife unfortunately lost her hold. He was called on to stop and take up his wife, but he pushed on, crying out 'Let the Devil stop and take up his own.' The dominie's horse sprang forward at an increased speed, and succeeded in winning the broose. Fortunately the wife had received little injury, and was taken up behind one of the more sedate of the party.

In the United Kingdom all Christian marriage services – even the most elaborate of all, the Roman Catholic nuptial mass – now allow a certain amount of variation in the way they are conducted. The Church of Scotland's half-hour service might be considered rather short for the focal point of the wedding day. The guests frequently spend more time waiting for the bride to arrive, or shuffling up and down the church steps while the photographer shunts them into the chosen poses. But the importance of the marriage service for believer and unbeliever alike lies in the briefest part of all – the few seconds when the groom is placing the ring on his bride's finger.

'They christen without the cross, [and] marry without the ring,' wrote an English courtier who accompanied James VI to Scotland in 1617. And in the early eighteenth century, Captain Burt wrote, 'They do not use the Ring in Marriage, as in England'.

Portraits of married women painted before 1800 very rarely show them wearing a wedding ring. This applies to England as much as Scotland, and we know that a ring was always used in the Anglican marriage service. Rosalind Marshall suggests that women began to wear their wedding rings in the nineteenth century because the rise in population and increased social mobility made it more necessary to indicate one's marital status. This theory fits in with the standardising trend of the Victorian age – in the 1800s the plain gold band became the only permitted marriage ring, and permitted only for marriage. It must stay on the bride's finger for the rest of her life.

Prior to the seventeenth century, Scottish rings of any value – whether intended for betrothal, marriage or as private gifts – are usually jewelled. After that date, plain gold bands appear, but not necessarily as a sign of marriage.

A Scots Guard piper accompanies the groom Ronnie Goodall with his new bride out of church in the 1930s. (SLA)

Before the Reformation there was a strictly observed procedure for placing the ring on the bride's finger. The priest blessed the ring and then passed it to the bridegroom, who used it to circle the bride's right thumb, second, and third fingers in turn while he invoked the three persons of the Trinity, and with a final 'Amen' put it on her fourth finger '*quia in illo digito est quaedam vena procedens usque ad cor*' (because there is a certain vein in that finger leading directly to the heart). The ring stayed on the bride's finger for the rest of the marriage ceremony – but apparently it might not remain there.

After the Reformation in England the wedding ring was placed on the bride's left hand. (Roman Catholics did not adopt this practice until the end of the seventeenth century.) The Scottish Reformers seem to have jettisoned the ring altogether for a time, until it reappeared on the right thumb. By about 1700 it had settled into its current position. The fashion for married women to wear their wedding and engagement ring together began about 1830. Perhaps this was an attempt at self-expression when everyone was wearing the same unadorned gold band.

Modern jewellers compete in designing rings that will satisfy individual taste without breaking the convention that they must be made of plain gold. Today's wedding rings are often intricately engraved or patterned with 'Celtic' motifs.

A traditional gold wedding ring made in the 1870s by the Fergusson Brothers in Inverness.

8
Feasting, Dancing, Bedding and Kirking

The first two activities will probably form part of marriage celebrations as long as the institution itself remains; the fourth has disappeared from our secular society; and the third was fading away even before the squeamish Victorian age.

In Orkney and Shetland, there was a short dance in the minister's kitchen immediately after the wedding – the minister himself kissed and led out the bride. The guests then walked to the 'wedding house', where the bride's mother or some female relation stood outside to welcome the wedding party. Over the bride's head she broke a large cake of oatmeal or shortbread known as the 'infar cake' or the 'dreaming bread'. The unmarried guests scrambled for the fragments, sometimes passed through a wedding ring, and slept with them under the pillow to determine their own fate in the marriage stakes.

In Orkney the name given to the woman who met the bride was the 'handsel-wife'. In times that are more distant she brought with her the youngest child of the district, the 'handsel bairn', who was put into the bride's arms. The child's movements there foretold if the first offspring would be a boy or a girl. In some areas of Scotland it was the mother of the groom who welcomed the bride as a sign that she was resigning her rights over her son to the new mistress of his house. At this point the groom lifted his bride over the threshold. She then approached the hearth, took up the poker and tongs, and made up the fire.

Some variety of this ceremony took place in every part of Scotland, but its precise timing depended on where the guests went for their marriage feast, for which there were various possible locations: the new home, the bride's father's barn, her parents own house, or a hired hall. If the guests went to a private house, the numbers might be so large that they had to eat in relays while the others danced.

As mentioned before, wedding presents often took the practical form of contributions to the feast. In the Islands women traditionally handed in poultry or baking and the men donated bottles of whisky which was drunk neat or spiced up for the 'bride's cog'. In addition, the guests often paid for the fiddler.

In such circumstances it is hard to distinguish between a normal community celebration and the 'penny (or 'siller') bridal', a prime target for ecclesiastical wrath for over two hundred years. The main difference seems to be that there were guests present who had no personal interest in the wedding, but were willing to pay to join in the party. George Penny explains:

> There were three different kinds of weddings [in the Perth area]: First, what was called a free wedding, to which only a few select friends were invited, and where the guests were not allowed to be at any expense. The dinner wedding, where the dinner was provided by the marriage party; the company paying for the drink and the fiddler; and the penny wedding, which was of frequent occurrence, and often produced a tolerably round sum for the young couple. The bridegroom produced a great quantity of eatables and drinkables, and opened the door to all and sundry. Each guest gave a shilling for his dinner, and paid for his drink, at a rate sufficient to yield more than a reasonable profit; so that, when the company was numerous, there were frequent instances of people who married without means, realising a sum from the festivities of the wedding, sufficient to furnish a house, or give them a fair commencement in trade.

Captain Burt reports that at penny weddings the bride went round and kissed every man in the room and 'in the End every Body puts Money into a Dish, according to their Inclination and Ability'. It is not clear whether he is referring to all penny weddings or only those held in large houses for a favourite servant, but this seems to be separate from the flat charge and sounds remarkably like the demands of later brides who 'jump the chanty'.

The down side of penny weddings was the lack of control over the guest list. In small communities, neighbours who had no inducement to keep the peace would become inflamed with the good cheer and revive old grudges. The violence could become physical, and occasionally even incite to murder.

In the main, however, the arrangement was of benefit to all – it was a big event for the community, the young couple profited, the guests had their money's worth and enjoyed themselves immensely. Despite the disapproval of the Kirk, the custom lived on. William Mackay wrote that he attended one just outside Inverness in 1870 'and contributed my mite towards the expense'. David Allan conveys the joyful exhilaration of these events in his famous painting, 'The Penny Wedding'.

Although the round of oatcake or shortbread broken over the bride's head was sometimes called the 'wedding cake', it did not occupy centre stage in the same way as the three-tiered iced confection we know today. That role was taken by the 'bride's pie', of which everyone must eat a portion. Here is Meg Dod's recipe, as given by F Marian McNeill, in *The Scots Kitchen*:

> Chop the meat of two calves' feet, previously boiled, a pound of mutton suet, and a pound of pared apples, all separately, till they are fine. Mix them and add to them a half-pound of picked and rubbed currants and the same quantity of raisins stoned and chopped. Season with a quarter-ounce of cinnamon in powder, two drams of grated nutmeg and pounded mace, an ounce of candied citron and double the quantity of lemon peel, both sliced thin, a glass of brandy, and another of Madeira. Line a thin pan which has a slip-bottom with puff paste, and put the minced meat, etc., into it. Roll out a cover for the pie, which usually has a glass or gold ring concealed somewhere in the crust, and should be embellished with suitable ornaments and devices, as Cupids, turtles, torches, flames, darts, and other emblematic devices of this kind.

The decorations of the modern wedding cake are also known as 'favours', and until quite recently the bridesmaids used to hand them out at the reception to the invited guests. Nowadays it is more usual to give them whisky miniatures or small packets of sugared almonds and chocolate truffles.

The hospitality offered to the guests at a nineteenth-century country wedding was a generous helping of their everyday fare. Lavish quantities of food and drink (especially drink) were more acceptable than exotic delicacies to people who had to win every mouthful with the labour of their hands. The main dish was a very substantial broth cooked from whatever local produce the guests contributed, usually poultry and mutton. In Shetland, wrote Robert Jamieson:

> The dinner consists of a savoury dish of 'stove,' made of five or six fat newly-slaughtered sheep, cut into small pieces with an axe, and boiled in the largest 'kettle' in the neighbourhood; it is seasoned with salt, pepper, and carraway seeds, and served boiling hot in huge dishes, around each of which are laid a number of cow's-horn spoons. The company are seated each opposite his own partner; grace is said; and fortunate is he who has secured a spoon with a

'The Penny Wedding' *by David Allan, 1795.* (The National Gallery of Scotland)

long handle, since in a few minutes the short-handed ones become encased in a mass of mutton-fat. Oat-cakes are eaten along with the 'stove,' and a glass of whisky concludes the repast.

In the North-East the broth (two kinds) was followed by rounds of beef and legs of mutton and puddings 'swimming in cream'. Anne Grant of Laggan (author of *Letters from the Mountains*) adds 'plovers, and a roast joint, and grouse in perfection', while in Mull in 1799, as well as the sacrificial sheep, Mrs Murray was offered cheese, butter, eggs and potatoes. Incidentally her account is one few to mention any form of vegetable. The Scots on the whole made great use of the potato as soon as it appeared, but they were very slow to add green vegetables to their diet. When they did the ingredients were usually boiled to death as part of their 'kail'. Fortunately, these greasy wedding feasts led on to hours of strenuous dancing.

At one time in Orkney and Shetland the revels continued for several days – whenever the dancers tired they withdrew for a few hours' sleep and then returned to the floor. Later on, and generally throughout Scotland, the guests contented themselves with dancing through the night, but it remained customary for the main wedding feast to be followed by others on different days to repay the hospitality.

Today's entertainment after the feast maintains the tradition that the bride and groom and their attendants should lead off the dancing. After that, there is no set procedure except to ensure a good mix of old and modern dances. In certain parts of Shetland the dance began with the 'Bride's Reel', in which the young woman danced with her maidens to say farewell to her single life, and similarly, the groom danced with his men. The tunes were ancient; it was said that one of them, the 'Aith Rant', had come from the fairies!

In some areas the bride's elder sister, if still unmarried, was obliged to wear a green garter at the wedding. In Fife the best maid tried to pin it secretly to the unmarried elder sister or brother during the dance. When she succeeded, the wearer had to keep it round the left arm for the rest of the evening. Near Glasgow the same relations had to dance the first reel without their shoes.

Although many people associate Scottish dancing with Highland bagpipes, a fiddle is more traditional for evening wedding dances, which for preference took place indoors, unless there was a fine moonlit night. David Allan's *Highland Wedding* pictures show Niel Gow, the famous fiddler, energetically plying his bow for the dancers.

When the evening was well advanced some unusual guests turned up at Shetland wedding dances. In Norse mythology Odin and the other gods may disguise themselves to mingle with human beings, so strangers are always welcomed. This is how Robert Jamieson describes the 'guisers':

In walks a tall, slender-looking man, called the 'scuddler', his face closely veiled with a white cambric napkin, and on his head a cap made of straw, in shape like sugar-loaf … filled with ribbons of every conceivable hue …. He wears a white shirt, with a band of ribbons around each arm … with a petticoat of long clean straw called 'gloy' …. Having danced for a few minutes, another enters, called the 'gentleman,' somewhat similarly attired: he, too, having danced, a third, called the 'fool,' appears, and so on until all [six] are in …. They are careful to speak not a word lest they reveal their identity, and not a sound is heard but the music of the fiddle, the rustle of the straw petticoats, the thud of their feet on the earthen floor … and the whispers of the bride's maidens guessing who the guisers may be.

89

All good things must come to an end. The final dance was the 'Babbity Bouster', and in Orkney the signal for departure was the bride's cog, a large drinking vessel made of staves of brown and white wood. The host proposed a toast to the health of bride and groom. The bride took the first sip of the mixed sugar, spirits, hot ale and whisked eggs and then passed the cog round her guests.

The introduction of the honeymoon is a custom which was brought on by increasing prosperity and the rise in living standards. Prosperous Victorians took a 'wedding tour', usually in Continental Europe. It extended to several months, much longer than a modern honeymoon, and the family hoped that the couple would have a certain interesting event to announce when they returned.

In the past, the majority of Scots resumed their ordinary lives straight after the wedding. The man would go back to his work, and the woman began her duties as wife and housekeeper. Apart from their new status in the community, nothing had changed. Those who could afford a holiday would spend it in visiting a friend in a different area of the country. Then their closer friends would welcome them home with the infar cake and a renewal of the wedding festivities.

Even a short break was unusual, and it was difficult for the couple to find any privacy once the festivities were over. For many years the wedding guests took a huge delight in following the bride to her marriage bed. There is a faint echo of this in the way that the modern bride and groom try to make their escape unobserved, but not so unobserved that their friends are unable to pursue them with old shoes and a final burst of confetti. (Old shoes feature at many points in the history of weddings.)

In days gone by the pair either departed with the agreement of the company or were spirited away in turn for the 'bedding'. The bride was undressed by her maidens and put to bed to wait for the groom. While this went on, in Orkney weddings the bride's mother took the hair ribbon her daughter had worn in her single state and burned it on a hot stone. Early visitors to Scotland often mention that Scots girls never covered their hair until marriage, and the 'snood' (or snuid) was used to symbolise virginity.

When the bridegroom entered the bedroom the rest of the party rushed in with him to indulge in boisterous horseplay, ranging from a mock fight to carry off the bride's clothing to 'throwing the stocking'. Whoever the

An unusual example of dancing after a Scottish wedding – the all-male 'Bhangra', unique to British Asians. (SLA)

bride managed to hit with her stocking would be the next to marry. In 1802, John Ramsay lamented the passing of this old custom:

> I came home time enough to the wedding of one of my tenants .... It is now the mode to marry privately, a day or two before the feast – no public bedding! no throwing the stocking! as in days of yore! all is privacy; love locks the door and keeps the key.

The best man carried a bottle of whisky with him and more toasts followed in the bedroom before the guests took themselves away. In some districts they dragged the young couple out of bed and made them sleep in the barn while they drank and danced the night away inside the house. The rough treatment was explained away as a lesson in humility, but it more plausibly fits in with the superstition that evil spirits would not spoil the wedding night if the couple's friends gave them a taste of hardship beforehand.

An alternative was to lock the bride and groom into the bedroom until morning. We learn this from an anecdote told by George Penny about the disaster that struck one wedding in Perth. The main dish at the feast had been a pot of steaming kail:

> On one occasion, the damsel to whom the preparation of the kail was committed, unfortunately, instead of leeks, put into the pot a quantity of a strong purgative plant, called horse gladdening, formerly used as a medicine for cattle. The mistake was not noticed at the time; but some hours afterwards, when the guests had ridden a mile or two on their return home, the dose began to operate as a brisk cathartic. Numbers had to abandon their horses altogether, and in order to be ready for any sudden onset, proceeded homeward with their inexpressibles [breeches] across their shoulders. But the parties who suffered most, was the unfortunate bride and bridegroom, who, according to the established practice, had been locked up in their bed-chamber for the night; and who found escape alike impossible, either from the confinement, or the unremitting attacks of the enemy.

The morning that followed the wedding night had its own cluster of traditions and superstition. Two common beliefs were that the first to wake would be the first to die, and that it was unlucky for the couple to show themselves outdoors before they had eaten breakfast.

Drinking from the bride's cog in Stromness, date unknown. (SLA)

In the bridegroom's case this was a wise precaution against the 'creeling' which took place in the Borders and Highlands. When he rose from bed some of the male guests seized him and forced him to walk with a creel (wicker basket) filled with stones bound to his back. Only the bride could release him, and *only* if she was satisfied with his exertions the night before. Then might she cut the ropes of the creel. Needless to say, she usually did so as fast as possible! Among the miners of Fife there was a less severe ordeal – on the first day back at work the bridegroom had to 'stand his hand' to his workmates or be rubbed all over with coal dust.

There was one more ceremony necessary to complete the marriage. The first Sunday after the wedding was an important occasion for every Scottish bride, for this was her 'Kirking Sunday'. There was no special ceremony – the bride went to church in her best clothes, with her husband

A Mr and Mrs Cameron, of Stirling, on their honeymoon, circa *1880. They had four sons.* (SLA)

93

at her side. She did not consider herself properly married until she had been 'kirked'. In Perth the bridesmaid and other friends escorted the couple and distributed bread and cheese to all that they met on the way. Among the Fife miners the bride and groom sat in the same pew as the best maid and best man, and invited a courting couple to join them.

During the next few days the wedding guests would call on the bride and groom with small presents. In the fishing villages of the North East the wives or mothers of the men sharing a boat with the groom presented themselves with basins of oatmeal or other domestic gifts.

One last point is worth a mention. Until the English fashion crept northwards in the nineteenth century, married Scotswomen kept their maiden names. Where necessary, legal documents referred to them, for example, as 'Jessie Gourlay, or Brown'. Before the national newspapers thought 'née' more genteel, Jessie went into her obituary notice as 'Jessie Gourlay, wife of William Brown'; and 'Jessie Gourlay' was inscribed on her tombstone.

Somewhere in Scotland there may still exist a trio of elderly sisters, all widows, who have notched up five or six husbands between them and even today are known to their contemporaries as 'the McKinlay girls', but they are a disappearing breed and when they are gone that will be the end of another auld sang.

9
And so to Gretna …

Confirm your Old Blacksmith's Shop reservation … and send us the £75 fee. The fee includes use of marriage room and changing facilities, and witnesses should you need them. We are happy to arrange the services of a piper for an extra £30.

So reads **www.gretnagreen.com**.

You can still get married at Gretna Green if you book one of six local priests and ministers to perform the ceremony. Since a Scottish marriage can be solemnised in any setting, they will marry you over the anvil if you prefer that to the more conventional marriage room. Of course, it is all make believe. There never was a marrying blacksmith.

The 1939 Act abolishing marriage by consent before witnesses (see p 9) was supposed to put an end to Gretna Green, but the mythology was too powerful. Couples flocked instead to the Registry Office in nearby Gretna town, and in 1991 a purpose-built registry was set up at Gretna Green. Thirteen per cent of marriages in Scotland take place in this small village just across the Border (so claims **gretnagreen.com**). Half a million visitors a year visit Gretna Green to re-affirm their marriage vows, watch a mock wedding, or satisfy their curiosity about Scotland's romantic village.

Strangely enough, the first Border marriages were those of Scots heading south. In the 1600s, they went to find an Episcopalian or Anglican priest who would marry them if their own minister refused for any of the reasons mentioned in Chapter 2. But this was a mere trickle compared with the reverse flow that came later.

The story of Gretna Green begins with an attempt to stop the trade in irregular 'Fleet' marriages in London. In the metropolis, there were certain areas outside the jurisdiction of the Church of England where couples could marry without any delay for banns or a licence. Technically, the marriages were clandestine rather than irregular; that is, marriage by a priest or minister that did not fulfil all the requirements of the law such as banns or public celebration. An irregular marriage was one contracted

Tourists and lovers continue to visit Gretna Green's Famous Blacksmith's Shop and Museum, taken from a 1920s postcard. (SLA)

without the aid of a clergyman – legal in Scotland, but impossible in England, where the two terms became interchangeable.

Round the Fleet and King's Bench prisons flourished about sixty 'marriage houses' marked by the sign of two crossed hands. They carried on a brisk trade with the aid of clergy who would marry couples with some version of the normal Anglican service in return for a suitable fee.

Only a small proportion of the people who used the marriage houses were bigamists or fortune hunters, but the possibility of fraud caused huge anxiety to the landed classes. They feared that the young women in their families might fall prey to the system or even exploit it to defy their parents' wishes. The Westminster Parliament tried to remedy the situation in 1754. Lord Hardwicke's marriage Act ruled that it was a felony to solemnise marriage 'in any other place than a church or public chapel without banns or other licence'. The penalty was transportation for fourteen years, and any such marriages were declared void. Another stringent clause decreed that no one under the age of twenty-one could marry without the consent of parents or guardians.

The law did not apply to Scotland, the Channel Islands, or the Isle of Man. The two last destinations involved a sea voyage (and in any case Manx marriages were soon brought into line), but Scotland could be reached by land without the hazardous delay waiting for a ship. In 1784 there was a half-hearted attempt to extend some of the Hardwicke Act to Scotland by forbidding ministers unattached to parishes to celebrate marriages in non-parish churches. This was rather like stopping up a mouse-hole when the roof has blown off. As we have seen, there was no need of a clergyman to make a marriage legal in Scotland.

Before Gretna became pre-eminent, several other places near the Scottish-English Border were popular marriage destinations. In the early days, eloping couples were as likely to go to Annan or Coldstream as to Gretna Green. Once in Scotland, a simple declaration was all that they needed. In and around Gretna Green itself various houses were used for the marriages.

Most people want more than a bald statement to dignify an important moment of life, and the landlords of the inns where eloping lovers put up were quick to provide it. Others seized the chance to set up a business that would supplement the earnings of their regular trade. They frequently got away with it for decades. Any one of them might be a smuggler, toll-bar keeper, tobacconist, or joiner, and they carried on their service to impatient lovers at a variety of locations in and around Gretna Green. There never was a full-time blacksmith, although the myth had already taken root in the eighteenth century.

The 'priests', as they were called, wore formal clothes for the ceremony and issued 'marriage certificates'. Many of the registers they kept still exist; and the entries were used as proof of marital status if a couple become involved later in some legal dispute.

Taking away the curlicues and extras added to impress, what the priests actually did was to provide the setting for a marriage performed *'per verba de praesenti'* (see p 9), *ie* a declaration before witnesses. Even this takes time; so just to make sure, they also provided for a contract *'per verba de futuro'*. The 1780 edition of Pennant's *Tour* states:

> If pursuit of friends proves very hot; and there is not time for the ceremony, the frightened pair are advised to slip into bed; are shewn to the pursuers, who imagining they are irrevocably united, retire and leave them to consummate their unfinished loves.

It is unlikely that enraged English fathers would be weighing up the niceties of Scots marriage law at such a moment. More probably, they decided that any marriage was better than the ruin of their daughter's reputation. This is plainly the case in Jane Austen's *Pride and Prejudice*, when the horrid spectre of Gretna Green hovers over the Bennet family and Mr Darcy organises Lydia's marriage to the odious Wickham.

In addition, the priests themselves wished to cover all contingencies. Compared with the number of marriages performed, there are very few instances of any dispute about their legality. At one place the 'priest's' wife took the young couple straight into a bedroom after the wedding and told them to lie down. This was only to satisfy appearances; she returned seconds later to whisk the coverlet off them.

The 1754 Marriage Act placed severe pressure on couples who found themselves thwarted until both parties had reached their majority. The most usual cause of elopement was that the parents had refused their consent, and the most usual circumstance that the young woman was under age. At this time upper-class Englishwomen married in their late teens. The parents might have sound reasons for their refusal; but they might also be acting out of sheer prejudice. The conflict and ambiguity implicit in each elopement explains why Gretna Green excited such interest in the public imagination.

Before the tourist industry developed, most of the marriages at Gretna Green involved people from the middle or upper sections of English society. There were some notorious scandals and a few cases of sheer villainy. The lovers reached their destination 'post haste' – that is, by exchanging hired post horses at the inns along the Great North Road. To prove she was eloping of her own free will, it was usual for the woman to order the fresh horses; a damning piece of evidence in an abduction trial of 1827 was that this had not happened.

Marriages at Gretna Green more than doubled after the opening of the Carlisle to Glasgow railway line in 1850. The 'priests' used to line up behind the station railings to compete for the young couples who stepped out of the train at Gretna Junction. For this and other reasons, local opinion began to turn against the whole marriage trade. (The Church of Scotland had loudly denounced it from the very beginning.) Henry Brougham, the Lord Chancellor, who himself had married after an elopement (although not at Gretna), drafted a bill to make a three weeks' residence in Scotland obligatory before the marriage. To avoid upsetting the Scottish establishment, who raised howls of protest at any move to change the marriage laws, the clause applied only to one of the parties, and not at all if they had been born in Scotland, or possessed a permanent Scottish address. Brougham's bill became law on 1 January 1857. The marriage trade at Gretna Green did not die off completely, but it went into hibernation for forty years.

Since marriage was so easily contracted in Scotland, there was not much profit to be made out of it from the Scots themselves. Something similar to the Gretna scene did however develop in Edinburgh and Leith in the 1700s. The religious turnarounds of the seventeenth century had left a number of ministers without a parish. As in every profession there were also those unable to cope with its demands who were 'outed' for drunkenness, adultery, or eccentric behaviour. Some of them scraped an income together by setting up a kind of marriage agency. They gravitated to places with a floating population where they could find custom and avoid detection. One who was caught even managed to continue his service from prison.

In the eighteenth century, Leith was Scotland's largest port and a garrison town. The Government discouraged marriage for army rankers, so the Scottish 'priests' provided an unofficial service. (Sometimes army personnel carried this out for themselves.) When the Kirk Session caught up with the parties concerned, details were usually too elusive to track down the celebrants; they concealed their identity by operating from the steep tenements of the Canongate in Edinburgh's Royal Mile.

The modern history of Gretna Green dates from the end of the nineteenth century. By then it was possible to travel to almost every corner of Britain on the railway network. Excursion trains ran to and through Gretna. Visitors began to show an interest in the romantic history of Gretna Green. Their search for the marriage place began to coalesce round the local 'smithy' or forge, although in fact there had been several locations.

In 1895 a local farmer bought some property that included the forge and decided to cash in on his acquisition. In the face of great local resistance he fitted it up as a 'Gretna Green Museum' and installed a new 'priest'. The marriage trade started up again. Then Gretna Hall, one of the old marriage hotels, set up its own 'priest' and blacksmith's shop.

The two establishments went into fierce competition and both advertised 'marriage over the anvil'. There was soon enough trade for both.

The new priests, like the old, did not perform an 'anvil' marriage – they were merely witnessing it. They covered themselves by insisting on a signed declaration that the residency qualification had been met. In many instances, this was blatantly untrue, but no one could call the 'priests' to account. Gretna Green flourished, attracting couples from Scotland and Continental Europe as well as south Britain.

In 1970 the British age of majority was lowered from twenty-one to eighteen; and a few years later the Scottish privilege of marriage at the age of sixteen became legal throughout the UK. Yet none of this has affected the determination of those who want to pledge themselves at Gretna Green. In 1996 over 4,000 couples married in its Registry Office, the only one in Scotland to show a surplus of income over expenditure.

10
Fifty Scottish Proverbs on Love and Marriage

Appreciation, caution, contradiction, exasperation, satisfaction, resignation – all are present in Scottish proverbs about marriage and probably in those of every country.

- *A are gude lasses, but where do the ill wives come frae?*
- *A bonnie bride is soon buskit.*
- *A dink maiden aft maks a dirty wife.*
- *A dish o married love grows sune cauld.*
- *A fair maid tocherless will get mair wooers than husbands.*
- *A gude man maks a gude wife.*
- *A gude wife and health is a man's best wealth.*
- *A kiss and a drink o water mak but a wersh breakfast.*
- *A man may woo where he will, but maun wed where his weird is.*
- *An auld man's a bedfu o banes.*
- *A reeky house and a girnin wife, will lead a man a fashious life.*
- *A rich man's wooing's no lang doing.*
- *A tocherless dame sits lang at hame.*

- *Best to be off wi the auld love before we be on with the new.*
- *Better a tocher in her than wi her.*
- *Better half hang'd than ill married.*
- *Better unmarried than ill married.*
- *Bridal feasts are soon forgotten.*

- *Dawted daughters mak daidling wives.*

- *He's a fule that marries at Yule;*
  for when the bairn's to bear the corn's to shear.
- *He that has a bonnie wife needs mair than twa een.*
- *He that marries a widow and twa dochters has three back doors to his house.*

- *He that marries a widow will hae a dead man's head often thrown in his dish.*
- *He that woos a maiden maun come seldom in her sight:*
  he that woos a widow maun ply her day and night.
- *He wha marries for love without money, hath merry nights and sorry days.*
- *He wha tells his wife a is but newly married.*
- *He woos for cake and pudding.*
- *If ane winna, anither will; sae are maidens married.*
- *If she was my wife, I would mak a queen o her.*
- *If you sell your purse to your wife, gie her your breeks to the bargain.*

- *Like Bauldy's wedding, there's nae meat but muckle mirth.*
- *Like blood, like gude, like age, mak the happy marriage.*
- *Live upon love, as laverocks do upon leeks.*
- *Love and light winna hide.*
- *Love has nae law.*
- *Love is as warm amang cottars as courtiers.*
- *Love ower het soon cools.*

- *Maidens' tochers and ministers' stipends are aye less than ca'd.*
- *Marry abune your match, and get a maister.*
- *Marry for love, and work for siller.*
- *Marry your son when you will, but your dochter when you can.*
- *Mony ane kisses the bairn for love o the nurse.*
- *Mony fair promises at the marriage-making, but few at the tocher-paying.*

- *Ne'er marry a penniless maiden that's proud o her pedigree.*

- *Say aye 'No', and ye'll ne'er be married.*
- *She wadna hae the walkers, and the riders gaed by.*

- *The man wha sits on the silk goun-tail o the wife*
  wha's tocher bought it, never sits easy.
- *True love is aye blate.*

- *Wedding and ill wintering tame baith man and beast.*
- *Wives maun be had whether gude or bad.*

Further Enquiry

Margaret Bennett's *Scottish Customs from the Cradle to the Grave*, an anthology of written and oral reminiscences, contains nearly a hundred pages on courtship and marriage, with much fuller extracts from some of the sources I have mentioned. Those in search of historical perspective should read 'Sex, Love and Getting Married' in Professor T C Smout's *A Century of the Scottish People*. His twenty page chapter ranges in depth over the whole nineteenth century, and a lot more. Details of the famous and infamous figures associated with runaway marriages can be found in *Gretna Green*, a well-researched and lively account by Olga Sinclair (Dove, 1997).

Many of the major Scottish museums display rings and other love tokens in their collections, while there are examples of wedding dresses in specialised costume museums such as Shambellie House, New Abbey, Dumfries.

Finally, buried among the commercial promotions of cyberspace, it is possible to find websites that carry useful informationabout getting married in Scotland. Try **www.siliconglen.com/scotfaq** and do a search for 'Scottish Wedding Information'. (Please bear in mind that these details may change.)

Index

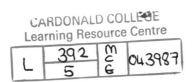